THE HIDER'S STORY

by

Jacqueline Gordon

I HAVE A VOICE ENTERPRISES
Peshtigo, Wisconsin

Copyright

Publisher: I Have A Voice Enterprises
P.O. Box 83
Peshtigo, WI 54157
715-789-2793

Cover design by Eaton Design Studios
Illustrations by Jacqueline S. Gordon

www.thehidersstory.com

Dedication

This book is dedicated to my wonderful sons,

Peter and Michael.

Their presence in my life has replenished my spirit

with blessings beyond measure.

It was for their welfare that I made the very first

changes that ultimately resulted in healing a

lifelong legacy of trauma and fear,

and breaking the cycle of violence.

The joy and goodness that they emanate

everywhere they go is a testament

to the resolve of the human spirit to survive

and rise above even the worst of life's afflictions.

Acknowledgements

A special thank you to David for accepting all of the hours I spent at my computer writing this book. I will always be grateful to my mother and two sisters, who have loved me unconditionally and supported me in whatever project I was working on, especially this one. To my dear friend, Jackie, who sat with me through many group counseling sessions and was always willing to listen and be a shoulder to cry on if I needed one in the most difficult days of my recovery process. Two co-workers, Steve and Pauline, both provided me with genuine encouragement and bolstered my self-esteem, which helped me realize I was a worthwhile person that had a lot to offer this world. And, finally, a special thank you to a multitude of caring teachers and others that gave me positive affirmations, making my childhood days a little more tolerable and leaving a lasting impression of hope for my future.

My editor, Eloise Rossler, gave me so many good suggestions to improve the readability of my book. A special thank you to Kay Eaton for her wonderful design services and to Sharon Kostelecky for her expert proofreading. There are many other individuals that encouraged me, gave me great advice, and helped me make this book a success. I greatly appreciate all of their kind assistance.

One of the most important lessons survivors of sexual assault need to learn is that we are not alone. There are many people that will stand by us and help us if we just ask.

Table of Contents

PAIN HEALS

The pain of the past still hurts
very much today.
It is real.
It feels as if it is happening again.

The big difference though,
is that the hurt that caused the pain
is not happening today.

Therefore, by drawing upon the courage
that helped me survive the hurt of the past
I can allow myself to feel
the pain today and not be afraid of it.

For only by feeling it in every part of me,
can I heal, become whole and live
in this moment,
today.

Preface: We are Me -- An Introduction

There are a few journeys in life that most of us would not choose for ourselves. For instance, I dreaded driving three hours to the hospital in which my mother lay dying; I wept privately inside my mind when I took my oldest son to his father's house because he chose to live there for a time instead of with me; and, I grieved when I dropped my youngest son off at college and came home to a quieter, emptier house. I asked God, "Why can't some things stay the same?"

"That's not how life is my child," God's still, small voice answered. "The most difficult journeys you will encounter will always require change. Welcome these new opportunities for growth with open arms by embracing the only thing in the cosmos that will always endure, my unconditional love for you, and you will know my peace."

One such loathsome journey began with the ending of yet another failed relationship. I sat on the furnitureless living room floor of a small, two-bedroom trailer-house that I had hurriedly rented and moved into the day before to escape, in secret, from an alcoholic and emotionally abusive man. At her request, my girlfriend's minister, a man I did not know, took the time to counsel me that day. I told him that something must be wrong with me. Every man that I had ever been involved with and loved had hurt me. I told him my life story as quickly as I could so that he could see my problem -- from a sexually abusive father, to a physically and emotionally violent first marriage that I somehow managed to get out of, and then all the men and boyfriends that came, used me, and left, leaving yet another huge crater in the middle of my already mutilated heart.

I told the minister, "I can't take this anymore, it's just too painful! I have to figure out how to change what I am doing so this doesn't happen to me anymore. What should I do?" The minister was kind as he listened to my blubbering and sobbing over the woes of my life. He suggested I seek counseling from a mental health professional and gave me the name of a lady of whom he had heard good things.

With shaky hands, I called for the first appointment. The therapist, Sarah, had her office in a large, sunny room across one end of her home. It was a pleasant room, filled with a variety of green plants sitting on a hardwood floor, wicker chairs padded with inviting floral cushions, interesting works of art decor expertly placed for effect, and low-volume classical music coming out of a hidden speaker. It felt like a safe and serene place to be. She motioned where I should sit and brought a note pad with her, sitting down across from me.

"Well, Jacqueline, tell me why are you here today?" Repeating the same story I had told the minister and posing the same problems, I asked her, "What should I do?"

She replied, "Jacqueline, you are very brave to tell me so much about yourself. I agree with you, you have had too much pain in your life. Sometimes when we are hurt as young children, we develop a variety of tactics to survive the ordeal. Unfortunately, most of us don't realize that once we grow up we tend to continue our dependence on survival tactics that actually end up sabotaging our adult relationships."

She continued, "If you really want to understand why you are getting involved in one disastrous relationship after another, I think what you need to do is to take a serious look at your childhood."

"Sarah," I interjected, "Why dig up the past? That is all over and done with and I just want to go forward with my life."

"I understand that, Jacqueline. I want you to go forward with your life as well and I believe you will only be able to go forward by first going back. What you really need to comprehend is that what happened to you, while it is all over and done with, is so much more than just a few memories -- you suffered severe emotional trauma. Even though we can't see the wounds, they are there, buried deep in your mind. From what you have just shared with me, I know these wounds are festering in your spirit and are affecting you today, Jacqueline. You won't get better by just ignoring your past because it's too agonizing to reminisce. Do you see what I am saying?"

"I guess so," I replied. "What will I have to do?"

"To start with, you are going to have to muster up all of the determination you can to work on recovering because it can be a long and painful process. You obviously had great courage and a strong will to survive what you went through and you will need that same tremendous courage to heal. Is it going to hurt? Yes! Is it going to be hard work? Yes! Is it going to be worth it? You bet it will be worth it! What do you think, Jacqueline?"

I timidly answered, "I know I want to get better, and if that is the only way, then I am ready to try anything." I made another appointment for two days later and she gave me an assignment -- I was to try to remember where I went to when my father abused me. I didn't understand what she meant and asked her to explain.

"Well, when children are violently assaulted like you described, they tend to go someplace in their minds to avoid the present situation they are in. Where did you go?"

I said to her, "I don't know."

"Just think about it over the next couple of days, Jacqueline, and see what you remember. We'll talk about it on Wednesday, okay?"

"Okay," I said with a sigh.

And so began the journey that I had tenaciously avoided for over twenty years. I spent about one year in counseling with Sarah, during which I was hospitalized for one month in an intensive treatment facility that specialized in assisting adults that had been sexually assaulted as children and were suffering from post traumatic stress disorder. A few years later I decided I needed help again and worked with a wonderful psychologist, Dr. Anderson, who had done a lot of work with patients similar to me. When I left his care, I felt more at peace with myself than I ever had. One significant strategy that Dr. Anderson had me do was to put my memories into drawings. He suggested that if I were to get the memories out of my head and onto paper I might be able to move on, away from the past into a more integrated present.

I believe the drawings were one of the most significant healing therapies in which I had participated. After I completed the art work, I wrote a story for each picture and discussed them in therapy sessions with Dr. Anderson. The idea came to me some time later to write a book about my past based on the stories of the pencil drawings. Thus, *The Hider's Story* came to be.

To protect the privacy and rights of individuals, the majority of names mentioned in this book have been changed.

HE, HIS, HIM, etc.

To easily know when I am referring to my biological father, I always refer to HIM in capital letters. I no longer refer to HIM as my dad because HE was never a "dad." HE was a very sick person that I happened to live with.

Meet the Voices

This book is based on true events in my life. From as early as I can remember until sometime during my fifteenth year, my father repeatedly sexually, physically, and emotionally assaulted me. To shield my psyche from what was actually occurring in those appalling and dispiriting moments, I fabricated a flawless parallel fantasy existence, complete with imaginary playmates and a log cabin nestled in a peaceful, mountain valley sanctuary. As the assaults continued and increased in prevalence, it became increasingly easy for me to slip away from the painful reality by fantasizing I was someone else doing something very different. I was able to live quite happily in a daydream life by visiting my psychological refuge, whether or not I was being assaulted.

Eventually, the *playmates* in my fantasy world took on a personality and uniqueness of *their* own. *They* became separate *voices*, nineteen in all, varying from one emotional extreme to another and varying in the jobs that *they* each did. The *voices* remain with me to this day. *One* gives me constant encouragement, *another* is angry and badgers me, *one* beckons me away to a safe, quiet place of serenity. Since the *voices* have always been a part of me, it seems perfectly normal for me to have all the constant, internal chatter.

On the outside, I manage to maintain one seemingly congruent personality that people around me know. However, on the inside the *voices* urge, comfort, argue, encourage, and conjure up a menagerie of ideas. Only *one* of the *voices* has a name: *The One Who Never Got Hurt is Dolly.* The *voices* do not have a distinct apparition, *they* are just *voices* with attitude. *They* change the way I feel or behave and sometimes have a lot to say to me about what I do.

To assist the reader, I have italicized all pronouns that reflect *one* of the nineteen *voices*, i.e., *"her," "she," "you," "they," "our,"* or *"we,"* etc. Me, my, and I always refer to the person that I am and are not italicized. Also, to clarify situations where a dialogue is taking place between two or more of the inner *voices*, I have used italics as well.

Throughout the book you will meet the nineteen *voices* that dwell in my mind. Usually, I refer to the *voices* as my inner *child* or *children*. Due to the complex layers of which inner *child* is cognizant of other inner *children* and which inner *child* is vigilant at that particular moment of the story, the reader will hear me refer to myself from the first, second, and third person point-of-view, as well as in the past and present tense. Sometimes this occurs within the same paragraph. In actuality, I may be talking about or directly to another inner *child*, but *they* are me -- *we* are me -- separate *parts*, separate inner *voices*, separate *temperaments* -- many *we*, one me, then and now.

While it may be disconcerting for some people, the fact is, there are many *parts* that comprise me and *we* each have an important job to do. No *one* is more important than the other, *we* are just different. *We* move effortlessly between each *part* so subtly and with such unnoticeable nuances that no one is aware of what is taking place, including *ourselves*. *We* are so dexterous that *we* can be totally different and yet totally alike in the same moment. Every once in awhile, however, there is a more obvious mood shift. People might, if they feel comfortable, comment to me about my weirdness. Usually I just laugh as I agree with them, "Yes, I am weird and I know I am not wrapped tight! After all, being normal, if such a thing exists, is highly overrated."

Actually, that is part of the beauty of how *we* survived -- no one knew. If they suspected anything, they might have found out about HIS secret -- a secret I vowed to keep. A quick look at *everyone's* jobs might help the reader visualize how each *voice* had an important role in my overall stability:

1) The Hider	Hid from HIM and hid the assaults from some of *us*, hid the assaults from the world for years.
2) The One That Never Got Hurt (Dolly)	*One part of us* that is protected from all harm.
3) The Pretty One	Accepts compliments from people.

4) The Confident One   Administers confidence to *whoever* needs it at the moment.

5) The Protector   Calms any of *us* that need calming.

6) The Ugly One   Takes on low self-esteem and body-image problems.

7) The Pretender   Pretends to be *someone else* to make life more tolerable, usually achieved through daydreaming and music.

8) The Truthful One   Discerns what truths can actually be told from those that can't.

9) The Runner   Just runs.

10) The Religious One   Pulls *us* out of hellish nightmares.

11) The Angry One   Takes on the anger so no *one else* has to deal with it.

12) The Liar   Just lies.

13) The Happy One   Jokes around, has a good sense of humor, puts on a happy face in situations in which a person is supposed to be happy or is genuinely happy.

14) The Shy One	Takes over when the situation would dictate that *we* not say anything. There was safety in silence.
15) The Dumb One	Takes on the insults of people.
16) The Smart One	Figures things out, accepts positive feedback.
17) The Sad One	Since all of *us* are mostly sad the majority of the time, *she* is rarely afforded a voice, it just depresses *us* more.
18) The Sexual One	Takes over sexual activities that are distasteful to some of the *others*.
19) The One Who Holds Us All Together or The Gatekeeper	Constantly maintains integrity and peace throughout *our* nineteen *selves*; guards the gate, beyond which *she* believes is insanity.

By compartmentalizing emotions or personality traits, each *voice* was given more strength, vigilance, and concentration when the situation called for it. Because I had to be constantly alert, carefully watching HIM and what HE was up to in order to respond quickly enough to get out of harm's way, I became extraordinarily sensitive to reading the meaning of eye movements, body language, postures, and gestures. I became a master myself in knowing what HIS intentions were.

Unlike most people, I created very specific connections, buffer zones and walls between emotions, it was safer that way. When I was unable to escape and it quickly became too horrible or terrifying, I simply disappeared altogether with *The Protector*. Also, I managed to protect myself as a whole; i.e., no *one part* of me had to shoulder the entire trauma when it was transpiring.

Okay, Miss Smarty Pants, 4.0 Einstein, herself, if you are so smart, how come you never figured out a way to tell on HIM? Huh? Huh? Oh, that's right, you are "The Smart One," and you have to show off with your big words and all your infinite wisdom. You still don't know anything about me! You're right about one thing, though, you are definitely not wrapped tight. People won't only think you're totally messed up, they will know we are.

Shhhh . . . Settle down now, she's almost done. We all do the best we can and she is only trying to do her best. You'll get to talk more later on, it's her turn right now.

We really must apologize for her, The Angry One, that is. She really can't help herself, you know. Hopefully, you will be able to be patient with her as you read our book. She does carry a heavy load. It's not that we intend to make excuses for her, it's just that we have become quite impervious to her ill-mannered antics and tend to ignore her much of the time. If we didn't tune her out, she would certainly drive us mad as she incessantly rambles on and on, ranting and raving about the same old things over and over again. If you took what she says too seriously, a person would think, "Wow, this person is totally screwed up and probably belongs in a mental institution somewhere!" But you have to remember, she is only one small part of who we are. She is just doing her part in maintaining our delicate balance. After The Angry One has her say, you will probably hear The Confident One giving encouragement or The Protector offering calming words.

Until I was an adult, I was never fully cognizant of these shifting personality characteristics. However, once I recognized them, I realized *they* had always been there and began to understand how *we* all worked together to survive -- it made so much sense. Over time I have accepted my different *voices* and see the beauty in each *one* of them. I am perfectly balanced, and wrapped tight or not, *we* are me.

Some readers will say, "We all have 'little voices' in our heads, you are making something out of nothing." Other critics may find the *voices* hard to believe and mental health professionals may each have a more specific prognosis as to what exactly is going on with me psychologically. Whatever opinions may be offered regarding the *voices*, I am content and satisfied with my perception of what they are and how they came to be. It works for me. In fact, once I accepted the *voices* as separate and unique entities that dwell in my mind, I felt much more comfortable, confident, and more surprisingly, whole. In other words, I realized I wasn't crazy after all, I was just maintaining my sanity in a rather creative way.

Jackie, Jacque, and Jacqueline

From time-to-time in the story, you will notice a different spelling of my name. I consciously changed the spelling of my name as I grew older and the spellings have nothing to do with the inner *voices*. As a young girl everyone spelled my name "Jackie." When I was a sophomore in high school and shortly after the assaults of my father ended, I began spelling my name "Jacque." It was a way for me to signify a major change in my life. I liked to think of myself as someone other than the little girl that was hurt by HIM. When I became an adult, I decided I would like to be called "Jacqueline," the beautiful name that my mother gave me.

HE Called the Assaults "Bothering"

How many times HE assaulted me and how many events I clearly remember are of no consequence. What is of consequence is the fact that HE did very frequently and violently assault me, that HE minimized HIS actions by referring to what HE did to me as a "bother," and that HE manipulated me with terror and fear to keep me silent in order that HE could continue HIS twisted, pedophilic behavior.

"Bother"
verb
To annoy, disturb, or anger, especially by minor irritations.

Was what HE did annoying? disturbing? angering? especially by <u>minor</u> irritations? No! Bother doesn't even begin to describe the mountain of emotions that I felt when HE assaulted me, nor does it describe the tremendous and varied impact it has had upon my entire life. To use a simile, if a fly "bothers" people and they shoo it away; HE was more like a Tyrannosaurus Rex breathing down their necks.

Whether the assaults started on February 16, 1955, or September 7, 1958, I can't say for sure; but the fact is, they started. What was the frequency? I don't know, but HE assaulted me often, beginning at an early age until I was around fifteen years old. The assault stories that are shared in this book are only a small portion of what happened repeatedly.

Some of the other assault events are hazier than these. Perhaps they were more violent and too horrible to remember. Perhaps the circumstances that preceded or followed them were quite ordinary and not worthy of long-term memory. Perhaps I disappeared within *The Protector*, one of the *voices* of my inner *children*, much earlier in the actual event of other assaults, leaving less reality for me to remember. Perhaps there were so many assaults that they just became blurred together in my mind, as these are events that happened more than thirty-five years ago.

The Others

While HIS assaults were by far the most damaging, HE wasn't the only one that hurt me. One person and then another and another harmed me. Each assault somehow reinforced one of HIS lies and what I accepted or didn't accept as truth about myself and my world view. Depending on the severity, each succeeding assault created another small crack or a huge hole in my psychological integrity. My reality, unfortunately, was that many people who were supposed to love and care for me were hurting me.

Where Was My Mother In All Of This?

My mother was the only hope and semblance of normality that I could trust. When she was around, I was safe, more relaxed, and sometimes, even happy. I firmly believed that I would lose her love if I told her what HE was doing to me. Naively trusting what HE said and imagining the worst cataclysmic scenario HE presented, my mother would surely cast me into a hellish exile -- a dark, bottomless abyss of shame from which there would be no reprieve.

The ironic tragedy of keeping HIS "secret" is the distant relationship I had patterned with Momma. The distance was easily achieved because she worked the graveyard shift for six years. From the time I was five until I was eleven she wasn't home or wasn't available because she was sleeping.

As much as I loved her and wanted her to keep me safe, I rarely shared anything with her other than casual small talk and whatever it took to get a few basic needs met. Hence, I was labeled "shy," and it seemed to me that Momma thought my quiet behavior was "normal" for a shy child.

Life situations changed and I grew up. Eventually my mother and I formed a wonderful adult friendship. She knew something sexually had happened between HIM and me, but I **never** told her all of what had really happened.

Why Didn't I Tell Someone?

HE was a six-foot tall man, HE was powerfully strong, and I was little -- only a four-year old girl when all of this started. HE scared me. Between what HE said HE would do to me and what HE said others would think of me, HE had quickly and easily brainwashed me into silence. HE was so good at frightening me. HIS methodical and harsh persuasion involved the use of well-concocted lies that were interlaced with an effectual indoctrination of an overwhelming and all-consuming fear -- complete and total fear instilled by a masterful manipulator ever so cleverly spun.

The fear was deeply and perfectly etched into my memory. It had been unrelentlessly nurtured until "telling" became a foreboding, a hideous monster lurking at the tip of my tongue that if released would swiftly and succinctly doom me to a life far worse than ever being "bothered" by HIM. I knew one thing for sure, and I knew that one thing extremely well: I must never tell.

In essence, I believed there was no one to turn to for help. Even though HIS predictions of my fate were I to tell on HIM didn't make sense to me at four years old, and even though I knew what HE was doing to me was wrong, the stakes were far too great. I was not going to risk self-inflicting my own demise by telling. Consequently, the only remedy I saw was to deal with the terror and pain of all the broken boundaries and promises in silent desperation.

There may be another factor, although a much lesser factor, that entered into the equation as to why I did not tell. In the upper Midwest region of the United States, there is a rather unique family philosophy that isn't necessarily the case elsewhere. While this philosophy has changed to some degree over the last thirty years, it was very evident in my family of origin. In essence, the philosophy says, "Stick by your family, no matter what. If they are mean, if they beat you, so what, they are your family, ya gotta love 'im. Work things out, forgive, heal, continue loving them, no matter what. HE's your father! Ya gotta love 'im, no matter what."

Ill-fated as the philosophy was, I heard the teaching from many people's point-of-view and accepted it as truth. My internal interpretation, however, was extreme. I was resilient, determined, and headstrong. No matter what HE did to me, no matter what anyone else did to me, I secretly vowed to myself that I was going to take it and survive, no matter what. So, keeping the "secret" became a huge job to me; I believed it to be my savior and I could not fail. It was an all-encompassing quest that became, paradoxically, my nemesis.

SECTION I:

THE EARLY YEARS

When we first drew The Hider, we believed that The Hider's only purpose was to find a place to hide from HIM. However, when we completed our drawings and looked back through them, we realized that her mission was so much greater. She hid all of our torment from The One Who Never Got Hurt. She hid the assaults from Momma, and for years she hid all of us from each other and from the rest of her world.

It was The Hider that was courageous enough to open the closet door to let these stories be told . . . .

1 The Hider

Where can I hide? Where can I hide?
HE's coming. HE's coming.
Quick, under the bed.
No, in the closet.
No, HE'll find us there.
Hurry up! Hurry up! Hide!

In Momma's room, under her bed?
No, HE'll look there too.
You stupid idiot, just find a place to hide,
anyplace, before it's too late.
Hurry up! Hurry up! Hide!

The big closet, I know, I'll go in the big closet.
Close the door softly.
HE's on the steps already.
Hurry up! Hurry up! Hide!

What am I going to do?
HE must not find me.
I'll crouch down on the floor in the very back,
behind one of those garment bags,
with a blanket completely covering myself,
and then, HE won't find me.
Hurry up! Hurry up! Hide!

HE'll never find me today,
no, not today, I'm hiding really good.
S h h h . . . still, be very, very still.

HIS hand is on the door knob opening the door.
Quiet, don't breathe, don't move.
The light is on.
"Jackie, oh Jackie, are you in here?
Come out, Honey, Daddy just wants to talk to you."
We know what HE wants and it isn't talk.
S h h h . . . still. . .
Oh, I hope HE doesn't hear my heart pounding.
In my head it sounds like a herd of
a thousand wild buffalo stampeding across the prairie.
S h h h . . . still, be very, very still.

The light is off, the door is closing.
Yeah, I made it!
Wait, HE opens it again
quiet, still . . . .
It closes again.
S h h h . . . still, be very, very still.

Take a deep breath
breathe again, slowly
calm yourself
S h h h. . . calm yourself.

You did your job well today.
Calm yourself
you are safe today.
I'll stay here until Momma comes home.
Just be still and calm . . . s t i l l . . . c a l m . . .
S h h h. . . calm yourself.

Initiation in Fear

Big city life in Milwaukee was not for my parents. They had grown up in the quiet country and wanted to be back home. So, in 1955 they bought a small farm nine miles outside of Antigo, Wisconsin. Their plan was to work the farm on a part-time basis to make some money from the milk cows, and then both of them would work on one of the large potato farms that surrounded the Antigo area. Even though the buildings on my parents' new farm were old and in disrepair, my parents were comfortable because they were in familiar territory. Gramma and Grampa Jameson, my mom's parents, lived on a farm just a half-a-mile down the road in one direction and Gramma and Grampa Harding, HIS parents, were just up the hill the other way.

There was a rickety old barn, an outhouse, and a small, two-story house that was minimally modernized with electricity. We had cold running water in the kitchen and a wood stove for cooking and heating the house. Since we didn't have an indoor bathroom, we had to use a stinky, old outhouse. Following a narrow, beaten-down trail with tall grass growing along either side, we would almost always come across one or more large pine snakes slithering along the path on our way to the outhouse or on the way back. Momma always made us open the door a little to inspect the outhouse before we walked in, just in case a snake might have crawled in there too. She said there were so many of them around because of the old pile of cow manure left rotting out in the barnyard for so many years, and with the river just across the field, the snakes had perfect conditions to thrive.

If Momma was home, she would always walk with me when I needed to go. My older brother just looked at me like I was some sort of moron if I asked him. I learned not even to ask HIM because HE would just hiss at me. And when the mean babysitters were there, well, I'd rather risk running into a snake than ask one of them to go with me. Because it was such a frightening walk for me, I usually didn't go there if I just had to pee and Momma wasn't home. Instead, I'd sneakily loot some tissues from the house, do my best to evade detection, and steal away to the colossal oak tree in the back yard, crouch down there and pee. The tree had a massive trunk that must have been about four feet in diameter and fifteen feet in circumference -- no one could see me from the house or from the road when I was there. At the bottom of the tree there was a large hole where I'd stuff the used tissues and cover them with old leaves or grass to hide them -- and I thought the squirrels that collected the acorns from the tree might be able to use them for their nest.

In the middle of the kitchen floor of that old house, there was a hinged door that led down to a small dirt cellar that was about eight feet by ten feet wide and about seven feet deep. The only things down there were the kitchen water pipes and drain pipes and a few things Momma stored down there, like the square metal tub we used for bathing, canning jars, which sat on homemade shelves, (the kind of shelving that was quickly constructed with cement blocks and some old boards), and a few other seldom-used items on an old, wobbly wooden table.

When supper dishes were done on Saturday nights, Momma would drag away the colorfully-braided, rag rug that concealed the door in the floor in order to go down to the cellar to get the square wash tub for our weekly bath. On at least two occasions when Momma opened that door in the floor, she screamed frantically because she saw a nasty old pine snake on the dirt floor down below. She'd holler for HIM to go down there, kill it and get rid of the thing. When HE came up from the cellar with the long dead snake at the end of a pitch fork, HE would swing the smashed snake's head in my face and hiss at me as HE walked by me to take it outside. Momma scolded HIM and told HIM not to do that to me.

Once the commotion had settled down, she got the tub up from the cellar and closed the door. Placing the tub near the warm wood stove, she would wipe it out with a rag and then begin to heat large kettles of water on the kitchen stove to fill the tub for our baths. While the water was warming up, we'd all sit in the living room and watch "Gunsmoke" on TV. Once in a while, if we were lucky, she'd have a treat for us like ice cream, popcorn, or my favorite, chocolate mayonnaise cake with fluffy-white frosting. As soon as "Gunsmoke" was over, I was always the first one to get a bath, and then my brother would go next -- she wanted us to be glistening clean for church on Sunday morning. While Momma was warming more water for herself and HIM, she'd get us settled into bed for the night.

The two upstairs bedrooms were very small, but had exceptionally tall ceilings. My brother, Richard, and I shared one of the rooms and had a bunk-bed to save space in the small room. Encircling the entire room was a narrow ledge made of wood that was about one foot higher than the door that came into our room. Where the wall met the ceiling several feet above the ledge there was another decorative board that was flush to the wall. By standing on the top bunk-bed we could climb onto the ledge and walk on it. The board was wide enough so that about half of my foot fit on it. The board at the ceiling level was mounted in such a way that we could slip our fingertips over the top and behind just a little bit, enabling us to have something to cling to as we maneuvered our way around the room on the narrow ledge.

On one of those fun Saturday nights when I was about four years old, Momma put us to bed, and as soon as she went back downstairs, Richard and I got up. We opened the door so there was enough light in the room for us to be able to see and walk on the ledge. We imagined we were cartoon super heroes as we bravely clung to the edge of a sheer cliff rising high above the canyon floor far below us. As I inched my around the ledge and was just over the door, the upper board abruptly pulled off the wall and gravity acquired control of my little body, launching me swiftly downward. The fall was obstructed by the top of the door -- I whacked it so forcefully that I mangled my bottom parts. Careening off the door, I resumed my descent and quickly crashed into the floor.

The loud thump and the ensuing screams brought Momma and HIM rushing upstairs to see what had happened. There I was crumpled up on the floor, twisting and moaning in pain. Smashing the door on the way down as I did caused severe damage to my genital area. I was bleeding profusely out of two seemingly deep gashes, so they took me to the hospital emergency room. No stitches were required, but because of the area involved, they couldn't bandage my wounds properly and were concerned about infection. They gave Momma some anti-bacterial ointment for me that needed to be applied four times a day after carefully cleaning the area.

Because walking and sitting were intolerably hurtful, I lingered in bed for several days after the accident. Climbing the stairs to check on me and then to clean and treat me with ointment four times a day became laborious for Momma, who was late in her third pregnancy at the time. Whenever possible, she would have HIM come upstairs to my bed to take care of me, but HE did things differently than Momma -- HE would pull off my panties and peer at my bottom for a very long time before starting to clean me.

One day when Momma had gone grocery shopping, HE brought me lunch to eat. While I was sitting up in bed, I noticed that the sunlight shining through the lacy curtains was creating interesting shapes and shadows on the bedspread. HE sat and talked to me as I ate my lunch and we conjectured what the shapes and shadows resembled. When I was done eating, HE took my dishes and set them on the tray that HE had brought them on which was on my dresser drawers in front of the window. HE pondered there for a few minutes with HIS back to me. Gazing out the high window,

HE bent HIS head slightly to one side and then to the other. In a few minutes HE brought a damp rag back with HIM to wash my face -- it was warm and very soothing. When HE was done with my face, HE said it was time to clean and treat my bottom. Again, HE took my panties down and eyed my bottom for a long time before starting to cleanse it. After HE applied the ointment, HE got up to look out of the small window one more time and then turned around to me.

Different eyes, different face, different DADDY. I didn't understand what the metamorphosed face meant, but I witnessed, for the first time, the transformation of my loving and caring daddy into an ominously debauched specter which was now lurking in my room. Without shifting his crazed focus away from my frightened, gaping eyes, HE moved HIS hands to HIS belt and unbuckled it, then HE unzipped HIS pants. I saw IT wiggling in my face, wiggling on my lips as HE moved IT back and forth. Again I scrutinized HIS face, trying to find even a tiny glimmer of my old daddy; but all I detected were those intensely startling eyes, devoid of anything familiar. HE was lost in his own obsession, engrossed in an unspeakable carnality, and I knew that I did not exist to HIM at that moment. HE was working my mouth open and I felt IT in my mouth -- IT was so big, IT gagged me and made me feel like I needed to vomit. IT took my breath away, and I feared HE was going to suffocate me. When I started to flail uncontrollably and gasp for breath, HE took IT out of my mouth. HE stood in front of me and began gawking at my bare bottom, all the while wiggling IT up and down until something creamy and white came out of the end of IT. I didn't understand what the altered face meant, I didn't know what the wiggling meant, I didn't know what had just transpired, but I did know it was somehow all wrong because it felt that way.

HE zipped up HIS pants and said to me, "Now Jackie, you must never tell your Momma what we did here today. You must never tell anyone! If you do, your mother will hate you. She will hate you so much that she will leave you. She will believe that you are a wicked, wicked child that doesn't deserve her precious love. She will kick you out of her home and make you go live in a children's orphanage with all of the other naughty children that got kicked out of their homes. You think those kids will be nice to you? No way. Those are the meanest children in the entire United States of America. No one wants them because they are so mean and they will be even meaner to you because of the terrible things your mother will tell them about you when she leaves you there. Your mother will kick me out of the house too, and it will be entirely your fault that your family has to break up. You don't want that to happen now, do you? You wouldn't want all of that to be your fault, would you? You must never, never tell." Shaking my shoulders, HE said, "Promise me you won't tell."

"No Daddy, I won't ever tell."

"Promise me, Jackie. This is very important to you if you want to be happy."

"I promise!"

"Okay. Now, let's get your panties back on. I've got things to do. I'll see you later."

After HE left, I cried awhile. I didn't want Momma to hate me so I decided to keep my promise to never tell.

In a little while I fell asleep and had a horrible dream. *I dreamt I was down in the dirt cellar. The door in the floor was closed from above and there were two other people in the room with me. One of them was HIM, the other person was a woman I did not recognize. They both were wearing long, black, hooded robes that were edged with red cording along the bottom of the sleeves, around the bottom of the robe, and all around the large hood that covered much of their faces. I was lying in the middle of the room on the old wooden, wobbly table with nothing on. My head hurt very badly and my vision seemed slightly blurred. My mouth had been gagged with some sort of a rag so I could not make any noises, and my hands and feet were tied down, stretched apart as far as they would go, making it impossible for me to move at all.*

The only light in the room came from a variety of candles. I could see the metal wash tub had been turned upside down to be used as a table, on top of which sat two more candles, an open book, and a dark colored bowl containing some sort of liquid along with a silver ladle-like spoon setting next to the bowl. The two people were whispering about me, but I could not make out exactly what they were saying.

HE walked over to the upside-down-tub table carrying a covered wicker basket and the woman walked to my other side. HE handed the woman the book and then set the basket down where the book had been. She began to read words from the book that were not in English, and then she started chanting something in a monotone voice. When she was done chanting, HE took the spoon, dipped some of the mysterious liquid out of the bowl. HE poured it over my body from the top of my head to my lower abdomen and continued from there down one leg all the way to the end of my big toe, repeating the same thing on my other leg. The woman read from the book again and chanted some more.

Next, HE took the wicker basket and removed the lid, revealing a snake. Grabbing it by the head with one of HIS hands and by the tail with HIS other hand, HE held the snake over the length of my body while they both chanted. As HE started to move the snake closer to my body, I woke up in bed screaming.

Momma was home and came hurrying up the stairs. I was crying and she held me for awhile. I told her I had just woke up from a bad dream. While she was comforting me, I decided that it was time to get out of bed and back to normal life -- I was not going to let HIM take care of me anymore. Then I told Momma a lie. I said, "Momma, boys and girls aren't supposed to see each other's bottoms are they?"

"No they're not! What brought that up, Jackie?"

"Well, Daddy is a boy and when HE puts the ointment on me HE is seeing my bottom."

"Oh, I see, Jackie," Momma said, "That's different. HE is your Daddy, HE's not a boy."

"But, Momma, HE is a grown-up boy, isn't HE?

"Well . . . yes . . . , HE is a grown-up boy," Momma replied.

"Okay, then I don't want HIM to see my bottom anymore. I just want you to put the ointment on. It is only for two more days anyway. Okay?"

"I suppose, Jackie. That would be okay."

"Thank you, Momma, that makes me feel better. Momma, I think I feel good enough now that I don't have to be in bed anymore. Can I get up and go downstairs now?"

"That would be nice, Jackie. Let's get some warm clothes on you and you can come down and help me make a cake for supper."

"Okay, Momma. I love you."

"I love you too, Jackie."

The next morning I heard Momma wake Richard to get ready for school. I always waited until the school bus stopped to pick him up before I got out of bed. Then I heard the front door open and close thinking that HE was going somewhere. I was surprised when I got up to look out the window to see that Momma was the one that had gotten in the car to go someplace. Shrugging my shoulders, I went pee in the overnight potty, grimacing when the hot, stinging pee gushed bitingly across the unhealed portions of the lacerations. I grabbed my dollies and climbed back into bed. No use getting up until Momma came back to fix me some breakfast was what I thought to myself. The past Christmas, which was actually just a couple of months previous, I had acquired two new dollies. One was a hand-sewn, cloth doll that Gramma had made especially for me, and the other was a beautiful doll that Santa had brought me. I played with them in bed pretending that they were talking to each other about what to do today.

Then, I heard HIS heavy footsteps stomp up the stairs. HE thundered into the room with a furious expression on his face. HE bellowed at me, "I thought I told you yesterday that you were not to tell your mother anything about our secret?"

I started to cry, "Daddy, I promise, I didn't say anything."

"You little liar," HE screamed even louder. "Your mother told me you were talking to her about boys and girls not seeing each other's bottoms. What was that all about? Don't you know she could have figured something out from that?"

"I'm sorry, Daddy. Really, I'm sorry! I didn't say anything about what you did. I promise!"

"Well, I'm sorry too." HE grabbed the doll that Gramma had given me, roughly pulling her right out of my hands.

"Daddy, what are you doing? Please give her back to me. Please, Daddy, give me my Dolly."

HE became more agitated and shouted at me in a booming voice: "You must never say ANYTHING to Momma about boys' bottoms and what I did. Don't tell, Jackie. You see this little dolly of yours? This will be you if you ever tell. I will tear you apart just like I am going to tear apart your little dolly. Don't you ever tell ANYONE!!!"

First HE ripped the pretty hand-made dress off of her and tore it into two pieces. Then, HE tore off one of Dolly's arms, HE said to me, "See, you won't have a right arm. Never tell your Momma." Then HE tore off Dolly's other arm and said, "See, you won't have a left arm. Tell your Gramma and then I'll pull off your legs, just like I'm pulling off your Dolly's legs. Then, last will come your head. If you ever tell, I'll pull your head right off, just like Dolly's head is coming off right now. Do you understand this, Jackie? If you ever tell anyone, ANYONE, you will die. You will die a horrible, slow, painful death that will last a long, long time. You won't die quickly if you ever tell. It will be agonizing and you will shriek out in pain as if someone would actually save you, but no one will come to save an atrocious child that breaks her promises. I will slowly, ever so slowly, tear your little body apart, bit by bit. Do you understand?"

"Yes, Daddy." I cried in shock at what HE just told me and at Dolly's pieces and stuffing all over my bed.

"Will you ever tell?"

"No, Daddy." I said weakly.

"Speak up, I can't hear you. Will you ever tell?"

"No, Daddy, I won't tell." I said louder.

"Remember your little Dolly here all torn to pieces -- that will be you if you ever tell. Now, promise me that you will never tell."

"I promise."

HE grabbed me out of bed by one arm, pulled my eyes up to HIS face, shook me real hard, and said to me, "Just remember, it would be all your fault if I had to do this to you. Now, you wouldn't want that to ever happen to you, would you? Let me hear it loud and clear."

"No, Daddy, I wouldn't," I whimpered.

HE shook me again and demanded, "Say it louder, say it like it is the last thing you'll ever say!"

"No, Daddy," I cried loudly now.

"You will never tell, will you? Say it louder so I know you won't lie to me again!"

"No Daddy, I won't ever tell. I promise!" I screamed at the top of my lungs.

"Okay, that's good. I believe you. Now I know that you'll never say anything." While I continued to sob inconsolably, HE gave me a hug and said in a much more composed voice, "You must straighten yourself up and give Daddy a big hug. You are my little girl and I love you. Stop your crying, okay?" HE rubbed my back in an attempt to comfort me and calm me down. HE said very gently, "You are a good girl and I know you won't ever tell, so I'll never have to tear you apart like your Dolly. Give Daddy a kiss and I'll go get a washcloth to wash your face off with. Okay?"

"Okay, Daddy."

While HE was gone, I hastily picked up Dolly and all of her pieces, putting them under my covers along with my other Dolly. HE shortly returned with a damp rag, softly washed my still tearing eyes, told me I was a good girl, and got up to leave. On HIS way out of the room, HE turned back to me with the wicked smile on HIS face that I had seen the day before. HE winked at me, pointed HIS finger at my head like a gun, moved his thumb as if to pull the trigger and said, "Bang! Bang! You're dead! Don't forget your promise, never tell anyone!"

Holding Dolly's pieces close to my heart and rocking her back and forth, I cried quietly as I said to her, "I am so sorry, Dolly. I should have not let go of you when HE grabbed you away from me. I am so sorry, baby. I'll take care of you from now on and HE'll never touch you again. I promise, Dolly. I promise." Then I picked up the one that hadn't been hurt and I said to her, "You are so lucky Dolly, you are so lucky that HE didn't touch you. I promise you on this day that you will always be safe because I will protect you. HE will never touch you. HE will never hurt you. Cross my heart and hope to die." I lay down on my bed and cried until I went to sleep.

Later, I was awakened by Momma, calling upstairs to me to see if I was ready for some breakfast. I said I'd be down in a little bit. While I was pulling on my pants and shirt, I decided I had to find a very secret hiding place for my Dollies. During breakfast, I asked Momma, "Do you have a box I could use? I need one about this big," as I motioned with my hands to show her how big I wanted it.

"You know, I think I have a box just like that." She left the room and quickly came back with an old boot box.

I said to her, "Thank you, Momma, it is perfect!"

"What are you going to do with the box?" Momma asked.

"Oh, I'm just going to put some of my things in there."

I quickly finished up my breakfast and went back to my room. I used the box to make a special little bed for my Dollies. Using all of the stuffing that HE had pulled out of Dolly for a mattress and one of Momma's dishtowels for a blanket, I gently put both Dollies in the box. I arranged the torn-apart Dolly as best as I could and laid the one that didn't get hurt next to her. Covering them tenderly with the remainder of the towel, I put the cover on and took them outside to their new home.

I hid them in a place that only I could find -- I crammed the box up in the hole of that oak tree out back where I went to pee. It fit there quite snugly. It was tight enough that the box couldn't fall down and up high enough in the hole that no one would ever see it unless they stuck their head up in it. Only I knew it was there. HE would never get HIS hands on either of my Dollies again. I would play with them only when I knew HE was going to be gone for a long time and no one else was watching where I went.

Each night before I went to sleep, I whispered goodnight to my Dollies who I knew were out in the tree in their boot-box-bed all by themselves. In my mind, I said to them, "Good night, Dollies, dream good dreams, you are safe and protected in our secret hiding place. I will see you again tomorrow." I imagined that they gave me a big hug goodnight before they closed their eyes, and then I would carefully watch over them until they fell softly asleep. Through my bedroom window there was one bright star that I wished on, "Star light, star bright, I wish I may, I wish I might, I wish my dreams come true tonight. I wish HE will never touch me like that again." Unfortunately, that was one wish that did not come true.

41

The One Who Never Got Hurt

Ring around the rosie,
pocket full of posies,
ashes, ashes, all fall down.
Only no one falls down.

They are all facing outwards in a tight and rigid formation
as if they were soldiers guarding an entrance to a sacred place.
In the middle of their impenetrable circle,
reinforced by the ever-present and ever-watchful Protector,
is The One Who Never Got Hurt, Dolly.

Watching Dolly is somewhat like looking into the surreal world of a
crystal snow ball.
She talks to no one
She knows no one but herself
She knows only the peaceful, carefree essence of the fantasy world
in which she lives.
She is forever protected from the harsh and dangerous realities of
the outside world, she is innocent, pure, and good.

Who are you, Dolly?
Why do they protect you so, Dolly?
Why do we say hello to you every morning of our lives, Dolly?

I'm Dolly, Silly,
They protect me from HIM, so HE doesn't break me.
You say good morning to me because you love me, Silly.

3 The Pretty One

Big eyes, long lashes, thick hair,
perfect white teeth, and a big smile.
Such a pretty girl,
these were the words I heard.

Just give her a few more years,
she'll be a regular knockout.
Such a pretty girl,
soon to be a pretty woman.

You have bedroom eyes.
What does that mean?
It means your eyes are beautiful.
Such a pretty girl,
with huge bedroom eyes.

Just wait until you start wearing makeup,
you'll be turning away all those good-looking boys.
Such a pretty girl,
you'll break many a young man's heart.

So ugly, so dumb, so shy, so sad,
how could we be
Such a pretty girl,
can't they see the torment in me?

Whatever words we heard,
we believed they were all
just useless chitter chatter.

Such a pretty girl,
whatever is the matter?

Most compliments were untrue,
people just trying to be kind.
Such a pretty girl didn't usually exist in our mind.
If HE was gone and posing no threat,
there were a few people that would
make us forget.
Such a pretty girl,
could she possibly dwell in "we are me"?

Funny, warm, loving, and kind,
Whatever Gramma said was true and genuine.
She was the only one who could possibly see
Such a pretty girl,
that lived within me.
Such a pretty girl, to Gramma
I'd always be.

The Mean Babysitters

In September following my fourth birthday, Momma went to work in the potato fields. She hired Ann, her sixteen-year-old sister, to take care of my new baby sister Maria and me. A few days after Momma started working, Ann's boyfriend came over to our farm, and soon Doug was coming over everyday around 10:00 a.m. As soon as he drove up in his noisy, sputtering car Aunt Ann would drop whatever she was doing to flit out of the house to meet him. They would start playing kissy-face with each other the instant he was out of his car. He gallantly gathered her up in his robust arms and promenaded her around the driveway, scooping and swooping her body around as if they were lovers at a grand ball, all the while bewitching each other with their young enchanted lips, precisely caressing, persuasively encouraging the covetous passion flaring within each of them.

When he was there, both of them hassled with me and treated me like I was an animal that they could poke and prod, constantly goading me to go outside to play. They habitually clamored, "Jackie, go outside to play. Quit being such a whiner and find something to do. You must be extraordinarily stupid since you can't entertain yourself for even a little while. Just go away and leave us alone!" If I were particularly stubborn, Doug would remove his belt and give me a harsh whipping with it. Then, he literally hauled me out of the house, slammed the door shut and locked it so that I couldn't get back in. I began to dislike the mean babysitters intensely, so everyday I started to run away from them, and there was only one place I wanted to go.

Up the road about one-half mile or so was where my favorite person, Gramma Harding, lived in a very small, original log cabin. There were only two rooms on the main level of the cabin and the upstairs area was just a loft where all the kids slept. If I could get there, I knew she would give me some fresh-baked bread with some sweet creamery butter and homemade blackberry jelly, along with a heaping portion of grandmotherly love and attention.

At first, the mean babysitters didn't even miss me. I would run up the road as fast as my little feet would flee, visit Gramma for awhile, and then go back home. Gramma would act surprised that I had showed up on her doorstep, but she was still pleased to see me. She picked me up in her strong arms, pulled me close to her and gave me a long, fond embrace, and questioned if Ann knew where I was.

Making up a quick lie, I said, "Well, of course, Gramma. You don't think I'd come up here without telling her where I was going, do you?" And since neither house had a phone, there was no way for her to call to check things out or to tell Ann to come and get me. My new routine began; as soon as Ann and Doug would kick me out, I would run away to Gramma's house.

When I got there one day, Gramma said, "It looks like you are here just in time to help me make bread. Do you want to help me?

"Sounds like fun, Gramma," I replied.

With eight mouths to feed, my Gramma made bread almost every single day while the others were away at school or working. Out came the huge ceramic bowl that she put the yeast into, along with just the right temperature of hot water and some sugar.

"How do you know what temperature is 'just right,' Gramma?" I asked.

"Well, when you test it, it should be just about too hot to keep your fingers in, but not so hot that they'd get burned if you left them in awhile."

"What do you do next, Gramma?"

"Well, we'll stir this yeast and sugar up until it's all dissolved in the water and then we'll put the lard in and stir some more until it melts."

As she was adding more flour I asked her, "How come you don't measure anything?"

"Jackie, I've made this same batch of bread so many times that I just know when everything is perfect. Now that we've got the dough mixed up, we'll put some flour on the counter here and then knead it for awhile, like this . . . why don't you try kneading it now, Jackie?"

"Okay, Gramma."

After we kneaded it for about ten minutes Gramma put the dough back in the big bowl and covered it up.

"What does that do, Gramma?"

"Well, the dough has to rise until it doubles in size."

"What makes it rise and why does it have to rise?"

"The yeast makes the bread rise, but I'm not exactly sure how it works. It needs to rise so that the dough stretches and stretches to become nice airy bread when it bakes."

"Oh, I see."

"You sure have a lot of questions today for such a very pretty, young lady. How about playing a game of cards with me while we wait for the bread to rise?"

"Okay, Gramma."

We played Crazy Eights until the bread grew really huge. Then Gramma shaped it into six loaves and sixteen buns. She covered them with a towel and said, "Now we have to wait until the bread dough doubles in size again."

"It really takes a long time to make bread doesn't it, Gramma?"

"Yes, it sure does."

"My Momma buys her bread from the bread man, but it doesn't taste as good as yours."

"That's because she works, Jackie, and she doesn't have the time to make homemade bread from scratch."

Finally, the bread was ready to bake and she placed the swollen loaves and buns carefully into the oven. Before long, the room was filled with the enticing aroma of baking bread.

"Gramma, it smells so good in here. They must almost be done, aren't they?" I could hardly wait to taste her delicious buns, still warm and fresh from the oven.

"Let's check them and see . . . well, I think we can take the buns out now, but the loaves of bread need to stay in longer." I eagerly watched her as she carefully pulled out the large, beautiful, golden-brown buns. As soon as she set them on top the stove, Gramma said, "We have to spread some lard over the top so they stay soft. When she finished with that she said, "Now, you can have a bun and put lots of butter on it."

I broke my bun open and steam came rushing out at me. I smeared the butter on really thick and watched it as it melted. Then I took the first bite. "Oh, Gramma, these are s-o-o-o wonderful. I bet there is no one in the whole-wide world that can make bread like you do."

"Here is some fresh blackberry jelly for the rest of your bun."

After lunching to my stomach's content on the buns, I helped Gramma with the dishes; she washed and I dried.

"Gramma, will you please wash my glasses for me? You always get them so clean."

"Give them here." She put the glasses in her hot, soapy dishwater, swished them around for a few seconds, and then dried them on her apron. To give them a final inspection, she held them up to the light. Turning to me she said, "There you go. Now you can see how pretty a girl you truly are."

"Thank you, Gramma, I love you so much."

"Thank you, Jackie! Now come here and give Gramma a big hug. I love you, Jackie." When I was with Gramma, I felt so pretty.

51

About that time, there was a knock on the door. Gramma went over to see who was there, and she said, "Well hello, Ann. Come on in."

Ann screamed at Gramma, "Jackie's been missing for hours! I can't find her anywhere . . . ." At that moment she saw me. I had been relishing my time with Gramma and hadn't even noticed that I had been gone from the mean babysitters for hours. She bolted over to me, grabbed me and said, "Jackie, have you been here all day?"

Gramma replied for me when I said nothing. "Yes, Ann, she got here about 10:30 this morning and we've been busy making bread. She told me you knew where she was."

Ann turned to me with glaring eyes. While shaking me by the shoulders, she said to me, "Jackie, do you know I've been looking everywhere for you? Here I thought you were drowned down in the river or eaten up by a bear out in the woods! You are coming home with me right now!" She pulled my pants and panties down right there in the kitchen and hit my little behind one time for each stinging word as she said, "Jackie, don't you ever do this again!"

She pulled my clothing up, grabbed my hand and tugged me out to the car. When we got home, I got another painful spanking and was scolded some more. I was told that I should never go up the road to Gramma Harding's house again and was confined to my room for the rest of that day.

That didn't stop me though. Whenever Doug would come over and I'd get kicked out of the house, up to Gramma's I'd march. Sadly enough, now they knew where to find me; but no matter how hard they spanked me, no matter how much they scolded me, I was going to go to Gramma's house. I was a determined four-year old kid. I just knew that Gramma would be kind to me and I had to get there, even if it was just for a little while.

On one of those determined days of mine and when I was just about to Gramma's house, I heard that obnoxious car engine I dreaded hearing every day start up back at the house. Turning around, I saw Doug backing out of the driveway, so I quickly ran off the road and found concealment in the tall grass. There was a steep bank so I carefully crawled on my hands and knees downward until I got to the bottom of the ditch, hoping Doug hadn't seen me. My idea was that he would check for me at Gramma's house, find I wasn't there, and then he would go back to our house. Once he was back, I would go to Gramma's for just a short visit, hurry home, and then just show up as if I had been around all the time. However, he had seen me dart into the ditch.

The car pulled off to the side of the road near where I had gone into the tall grass. I heard Doug get out of the car and slam the door shut -- I could tell he was very near to me.

"Jackie! Jackie! I know you are hiding in the grass. I saw you go in there. Come out right now!"

Oh no! He knows I'm here. I'm not going to get up. I'll just wait here and maybe he'll give up.

"Jackie! Jackie! I know you're in there. Come out right now, dammit!" The trunk of the car opened. I heard a zipper and then the clanking sound of metal against metal. "Jackie! Come out of the ditch right now! I've got a gun! Come out of there right now!"

When he said "gun," my anxiety was similar to grabbing hold of Grampa's electric fence and not being able to let go -- I thought I was done. He shot the gun and there was a huge bang as it fired.

"God dammit, Jackie, if you don't come out of that ditch right this second, I'll shoot into the grass until I hit you. You'll be dead, and then you won't be able to run away anymore."

Oh, no! He's going to kill me! I immediately stood up, waving my arms fearfully above my head and hollered, "Here I am. Please don't shoot me! I'll come out!" My legs were trembling so nervously that I could barely manage to climb up the steep incline of the ditch. When I stumbled up onto the shoulder of the road, he ran over to me, yanked me by the arm, gave me the most hurtful spanking ever, and harshly hurled me into the front seat of his wretched car. All the way back to the house he blared profanities at me, swearing that if I ever ran away again he would tie me up to the tree in the front yard and use me for target practice with his new shotgun. Even though I hated them both more than ever, Doug had scared me enough that I never ran away again. I spent most of my time back behind the oak tree playing with my Dollies until HE and Momma came home from the potato fields.

Shortly after that, Ann announced to everyone that she had accepted Doug's proposal to get married and that they would be moving to Oregon right after their wedding in three weeks. Since they were busy making wedding arrangements and moving plans, they were no longer worried about me or what I was doing. I didn't bother them either because I knew they would just yell at me. Besides, they were leaving me for good and I was feeling a great sense of relief knowing that they wouldn't be babysitting for me anymore. And who would get to take care of my sister and me for the rest of that potato season? My favorite gramma, Gramma Harding!

Momma Worked Nights

In early January 1959, we moved from our remote country farm to New Holstein, a small city of about two thousand souls, where HE and Momma were both hired for assembly-line work at Tecumseh, a large manufacturing plant that made small engines. Getting out of the potato fields and moving to town (albeit a small town) was exciting for Momma. After all, life on the farm didn't work out as well as they had hoped, and their families still wouldn't be too far away from the new town.

"No more dirt, no more walking all day behind a tractor, and no more standing for hours in a cold warehouse sorting through all the rotten potatoes," is what Momma said. "Our house in town will have indoor plumbing and there will be more money for us too, with both of us working good, decent-paying jobs."

At first, both HE and Momma worked second shift, from 3:00 p.m. until 11:00 p.m. They hired Donna, a high school senior, to watch us. One evening, before we were even completely unpacked from our recent move, they arrived home from work to an unexpected, disturbing event.

Donna was asleep with me on the couch in the living room. We both woke up when Momma gently nudged Donna; she got up and started getting ready to go home. Momma went in to check on Maria, who was not quite two years old yet and discovered that her baby was not there! HE was just about to leave with Donna to take her home when Momma came rushing out of Maria's room. "Donna," she gasped, "Maria is gone! Where is she?"

Donna quizzically replied, "What? I put her to bed at nine o'clock and she went right to sleep."

Momma, becoming more exasperated, said loudly, "Well, she's not there now! Where is she?"

Donna didn't have an answer so Momma directed each one of us to a different area of the house to search and said with watery eyes, "Tear the room apart if you need to, but find my baby!"

All of the lights in the house were switched on as we moved methodically from room to room, searching for our precious little one. We crawled under the beds, dug through the closets, rearranged the living room furniture, moved the draperies away from the windows, checked in the bathtub, peered into even the ridiculously small drawers that a baby could never fit into, and examined every cupboard in the kitchen. After carefully scrutinizing every nook and corner in the entire house, Maria was not to be found anywhere. Momma was frantic now. Tears were welling out of her eyes as she cried, "Oh, my God! Where is my baby? Where is she? WILEY!" she commanded HIM, "Call the police, NOW!"

We were still desperately searching for her when the police arrived. Quickly, the policemen questioned my nearly-hysterical mother, Donna, and HIM to find out what had happened. One of the policemen went outside to look around in the snow for any tracks that might give them a clue. Because there had been a storm earlier that evening and the freshly fallen snow was still being whipped around by a fierce wind, they were worried that they might not be able to see anything; and with nothing on but her pajamas, Maria could easily freeze to death if she were to have wandered outside in the blustery cold, winter air. HE and the other policeman stood in the kitchen talking about the situation. Momma led Donna, Richard, and me into the living room to instruct us to continue looking around the house for her baby.

With all of the commotion in the house and Momma cranking out loud orders to everyone, Maria must have been startled. All of a sudden, my brother and I heard soft whimpers coming from her room. We walked in there and heard her, but couldn't see her. As we searched around and moved toward her cries, we called out, "We found her! We found her!" Richard picked her up and even before he had her nestled in his arms, Momma was there beside us.

"Oh, my God. Thank you! Thank you, Lord. My baby, oh, my baby!" Momma's anxious frown instantly softened as she pulled her baby close to her bosom and rocked her from side to side. We all rejoiced, including the two policemen, nervously chuckling with Momma as we realized what had happened.

Apparently, Maria had crawled out of her bed after Donna had put her down and had fallen into a large-sized moving box that was at the end of her crib. The flaps of the box naturally flipped back up after Maria was in there, and since she was unable to get out, she just lay down on the unpacked clothing in the bottom of the dark, warm box and went to sleep.

Well, Momma declared that she was never, ever, going to have another babysitter. Almost losing her baby was more than she could endure and she never wanted to experience that again. So she started working a different shift than HE did in order that one or the other of them would be home with her children at all times.

The new schedule was ideal according to Momma. She could be home in time to feed my brother and me breakfast before sending us off to school, take naps during the day whenever Maria took her naps, get all of her cleaning chores done, spend some time with us after school, make supper for us, and lie down to rest about six o'clock in the evening until it was time for her go to work at eleven. Momma followed this schedule for about five years until Maria was in second grade and she had her fourth child, another daughter, Rebecca.

HE started working the day shift, which started at 7:00 a.m. and ended at 3:00 p.m. When Momma went to bed, we had to do the dishes, do our homework, and then we could watch TV until our bedtime which was at nine o'clock. Usually HE would be asleep in the chair by the time we went into the living room to watch television so we could watch whatever we wanted on the two channels that came in on our little black and white TV. Up until bedtime HE was, to some extent, a regular father. After Momma went to work, however, HE changed and nothing was predictable.

HE would stealthily creep into my room as if HE were a wild beast stalking HIS prey. I would be awakened as I felt HIM begin to move the covers that lay over my little body and HIS offensive, brutish hands pulled at my pajamas. Always struggling, always fighting, and always an endeavor in futility, I desperately attempted to escape or to avert the assault. Inevitably HIS strong hand would quickly cover my mouth and HE would say, "I have a snake in my pocket, and if you are not still and quiet right this instant, I'll put it in this bed with you." My eyes would bulge wide open with fright as I gave up the exhaustive, ineffectual fight, and once more relinquished my power to HIM.

In time, I trained myself to wake up when Momma was getting ready for work. As soon as she left, I would crawl under my bed or sneak into the closet. Sometimes I would sleepily stumble out of my room and find a hiding place elsewhere in the house. HE'd be walking around searching for me in the dark, "Jackie, oh Jackie. Where are you, Honey? Come on out now and go to bed." Of course, I would never willingly come out from my hiding place, but if HE searched long enough, HE was usually able to locate me.

On those occasions when HE did catch me, HE would lug me back to bed as I vehemently resisted. Equipped with the flashlight HE had used to hunt me down, HE would frequently examine my private area as if it were the first time HE had ever seen it, touching me with HIS vile hands or harsh tongue and repeating the same thing with my not yet formed breasts, HE'd repeat the motions of HIS loathsome routine. Sometimes, HE would disappear out of the room for awhile, returning shortly to say something repugnant about how Maria's body, (who was four years younger than I), compared to mine. I dreaded and hated the touch of HIS hand on my body's private parts; it was extremely repulsive. Over and over again HE would come into my room after Momma had left for work and over and over again it felt so extremely wrong for HIM to be touching me like that.

In HIS eyes I continued to see the frightening evil skulking there that knew no boundaries, that knew no love, that knew only one thing. HE didn't care at all that HE was hurting me, and nothing mattered to HIM when HE was in that trance-like state except getting what HE wanted, however HE wanted to get it.

When finished with HIS evil deed, HE would always say something to reinforce the fear, "Now don't you be telling your Momma anything about this. You know she will hate you and will leave you and you won't have a family anymore. They will all think you are a terrible, shameful little girl that doesn't deserve any love. You don't want these awful things to happen, do you, Jackie?"

I would give HIM the answer HE had taught me, "No, Daddy. I won't tell."

Then HIS eyes would relax and return to their normal appearance. HE would give me a big hug and say, "You are Daddy's oldest and most special daughter. Now go to sleep. I love you." It seemed as if HE had no conscience about what HE was doing, as if it were as commonplace as taking a stroll down the street on a sunny day. Nothing to worry about, nothing to fret over. We were just an everyday, average family, living normally and happily in a quiet, little town. HE was completely uncognizant of the havoc HE was inextricably forging in my young mind.

SECTION II:

THE ELEMENTARY YEARS

 My elementary years were filled with negative body images, terror, and trying to maintain my sanity. More and more relatives abused me in one way or another, school peers were cruel, and HE was relentless.

4 The Confident One

You can do it, you can, I know you can!
I told The Runner that she could be
a great Olympian if she practiced enough.
I told her she should go outside and start running
to practice for Olympic trials.
You must run and run and run,
and so, she did.

You can do it, you can, I know you can!
She ran up and down the long driveway in front of our house.
Back and forth, and back and forth,
even in the coldest and darkest of winter nights.
Her breath would get labored,
her legs would ache,
her hands would become numb from the cold,
but she would keep on running to build
her speed,
her strength,
her endurance.
The Runner maintained a four-year record at her high school
for the girls' 400 yard dash.

You can do it, you can, I know you can!
I told The Pretender she could be a renowned concert pianist.
I told her all she had to do was
practice, practice, practice, and practice some more.
and so, she did.

You can do it, you can, I know you can!

She would play the piano faithfully every day for an hour or more,
practicing all of her scales and the Hanon fingering pieces.
Up and down the scales and up and down the scales she would play.

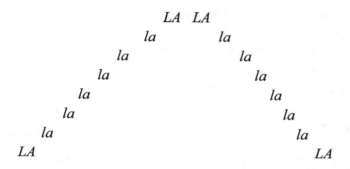

```
                LA   LA
           la          la
         la              la
       la                  la
     la                      la
   la                          la
 la                              la
LA                                 LA
```

Faster and faster she would go,
building her finger strength
building her dexterity.
Chopin's waltz, <u>Grande Valse brillante, Op. 18</u>,
all thirty-six pages of it were memorized by The Pretender.
She played the waltz at her senior-year recital
and was slotted as the grand finale.
HE came to hear us play, but Momma did not.

You can do it, you can, I know you can!
I told The Religious One that she could become a compassionate
missionary
to a far away, foreign land.
I told her all she needed to do was
pray, pray, and pray some more every day,
And so, she did.

You can do it, you can, I know you can!
Go to church regularly,
read your Bible,

commit Bible verses to memory -- as many as you can,
and go to missionary school after high school.
And so, she did.

You can do it, you can, I know you can!
She worked at church,
she played the piano for worship services,
she was a leader of the youth group,
she was a summer missionary for two summers,
she worked in vacation bible schools,
she took lessons to learn how to interpret church services for the
deaf,
she did everything I told her to do to prepare to be a missionary,
including going to a church school after high school.
The Religious One graduated from
Southern Nazarene University, Magna Cum Laude.

You can do it, you can, I know you can!
I told her she would offer Jesus to save
the lost souls of countless native people.
Upon return to the United States, The Religious One
would give reports to churches across the entire country
about all the people that were saved,
of all her trials and tribulations in a foreign and hostile land.
She would conclude her fantastic reports by
modestly telling them how the Lord Jesus was
with her every step of the way,
offering great blessings
and heavenly rewards for her selfless mission work.
She did not become a foreign missionary, but
has always worked in churches in her locale.

You can do it, you can, I know you can!
I told The Pretty One she could become a famous svelte runway
model, modeling the most chic clothing or adorning magazine
covers with those huge dramatic eyes of hers
that are so longing and so inviting
as if to ask people to look through them
to see deep into her soul.

You can do it, you can, I know you can!
I told The Smart One that she could do anything she wanted if she
put her mind to it.
You can be the first woman astronaut,
a doctor,
a writer,
a teacher,
an actor,
an executive secretary,
a hairdresser,
anything you want, just go for it with all you've got and make it
happen.
Make it happen -- the world is yours for the asking.

You can do it, you can, I know you can!
I told The Shy One, just ask.
That is the message she needed to hear.
Just ask the question, nothing bad will happen,
just open your mouth and
speak.

Sometimes it took an hour or more of encouragement
to get her to open up to ask one simple question.
Sometimes, she never did speak her mind.
She was so afraid.

You can do it, you can, I know you can!
We first heard it from HIM, but we didn't care.
It worked for us.
You can do it, you can, I know you can!

You Can Do It, You Can! I Know You Can!

Frequently, we would all get in the car and drive three hours to Antigo to visit the grandparents for the weekend. My favorite part of the ride was having a hamburger, french fries, and a chocolate shake at McDonald's on Highway 29 in Green Bay -- it was the only McDonald's that existed, as far as I knew, in the early 1960's. Each time we went there, I watched the "millions sold" sign numbers get higher and higher and thought the people that worked there must be very busy.

On one particular visit to the farm in the summer, it was hay baling time. Grampa Jameson farmed by himself and needed help getting the hay in, so we went up north to help him. Earlier in the week, Grampa had mowed and raked the hay so that it would be ready to be baled on the weekend. HE and Grampa would get it baled and into the barn on Saturday and Sunday. Friday night, however, the weather report predicted very bad thunderstorms for all of Saturday night and continuing into Sunday. Grampa didn't want his hay to rot, so they made a plan to get all of the baling done on Saturday. That meant all of us would need to pitch in.

When HE decided that I should drive the tractor to help bale hay, I began to cry.

"I can't drive a tractor, I'm only six!"

HE pointed up at the sky and said, "Jackie, see those clouds? We've got to get this hay baled <u>today</u>. The rain is coming tonight and it will ruin any hay left on the fields. Grampa won't have enough hay to feed his cows through the winter. You see, I need everyone helping and doing their part to get this job done. Do you understand?"

Still crying, I pleaded, "Daddy, I'm only six, I can hardly reach the pedals. How do you expect me to drive a tractor?"

He told me, "You can do it, you can, I know you can. I'll show you how!"

71

Going down the first row, HE quickly showed me how to steer, how to stop, and how to turn around to go down the next row. After these brief instructions, HE put the tractor in the lowest gear, let the clutch out, pointed the tractor straight down the long row of cut alfalfa there in front of us and then jumped off. I was on my own.

HE turned to me and said, "You can do it, you can. I know you can."

At first, I was so scared -- I held onto that steering wheel so tight that my knuckles ached as they turned from their normal pinkish beige color into a ghastly white. However, by the time we started down the third row, I had begun to relax a little as I thought to myself, "Wow, I made it down two rows all by myself. I can do this. I can, I know I can!" After that, I drove that tractor straight down those rows with my head held high, thinking I was something special as the bales continued to be born out of the back of hay-baler behind me. The hay got stacked higher and higher as HE piled the two by four foot bales of hay in a precise, crisscross pattern, starting at the back of the wagon and slowly working HIS way forward and upward as more and more bales materialized. Before we knew it, the wagon was full and we had to go unload it in order to continue.

My brother and Momma worked on another tractor baling hay in the field on the other side of the river, and Grampa and my Aunt Emily worked in the field across the road from the farm. Gramma stayed at the house to watch Maria. When we finally came together just before supper, everyone was exhilarated from the rush of having to hurry; yet, exhausted from the hot, humid, and monotonous work. They all told me what a wonderful job I had done steering the tractor.

HE told me, "See, you did drive that big tractor all by yourself. I knew you could." I was so proud, I had done it!

The next morning before anyone else was up, HE woke me and told me to get dressed to go for a tractor ride with HIM. HE was going out into the hills to get the cows down for milking. We started up the tractor and rode to the tool shed that was near the gate to the field that we were going to be entering. HE stopped the tractor, put it in park, got down, and told me to wait a minute. HE had to get something out of the tool shed. While I waited for him to come back, I thought about all of the exhilaration of the previous day and felt proud of myself once more for driving that tractor straight down those rows. I yawned and stretched, then pulled my sweater a little tighter around me. It was cold outside, a cloudy and damp morning, after all the rain that had fallen during the night. HE came back, threw a gunnysack and a pitchfork on the wagon we were pulling and we took off to the hills to get the cows.

The cows' pasture included a wooded and hilly eighty-acre area behind the farm. We drove a long way following the trail through the woods until we found the cows way at the back end, where there was more pasture for them to graze. HE picked me up and had me stand on the wagon while HE went around shooing the cows down the trail that led back to the farm. After the last one was prodded away, HE jumped up on the wagon with me. HE had that wild, scary look in HIS eyes that I now recognized as a sign of trouble. HE grabbed me very quickly before I had a chance to jump down and start running. I kicked, I screamed, I hollered, but HE just ignored my protests and went on with what HE was doing. HE told me, "Jackie, shut up and be still right now!" While still hanging onto me with one hand, HE moved us across the wagon to within reach of the gunnysack that HE had thrown there earlier. Then HE said to me, "Jackie, do you know what I have in here?"

I shrugged my shoulders and yelled, "I don't know and I don't care. Just let me go!" While I was still wiggling and squirming, trying to get away, HE managed to maintain HIS grip on me and the gunnysack.

"I'll tell you what's in it! I have a huge pine snake in here. This gunnysack is big enough for you and the snake. If you don't shut up and settle down right now, I am going to put you in there with it. Do you understand?"

With that statement, I immediately became still. I could see something moving in the gunnysack, and I started to tremble and cry, "No, Daddy, no! Please, Daddy, please! I'll be still now, I'll be quiet. Please take that thing away from me. I'll be still. I promise."

Once I had settled down, HE set the gunnysack down at the other end of the wagon, pulled my pants and panties down, glaring at me while HE did HIS routine. Finished, HE jumped up and grabbed the gunnysack. I was still partially undressed with my pants and panties down around my ankles which made it almost impossible for me to move. After I saw HIM grab the gunnysack, I became terrified and started screaming, "No, Daddy, no! Please don't! Get that thing out of there. Please, Daddy, please!"

Not listening to me, HE took the pitchfork and forcefully stuck it into the side of the bag a couple of times, stabbing the snake. Then HE opened the bag, used the pitchfork to pick up the dying snake, and stood with it at the other end of the wagon. HE hissed at me as HE moved the pitchfork back and forth, the snake still jerking. Then HE said, "Jackie, you won't ever tell, will you?"

"No, Daddy, I won't tell, I promise. Please get that thing out of here! Please, Daddy, I won't ever tell ANYONE."

"H i s-s-s, h i s-s-s," HE teasingly said to me still waving the snake. "No, I'm sure you won't tell because if you do, you know what will happen. Don't you Jackie?"

"Yes, Daddy, I know what will happen."

"And, what is that, what will happen?"

"You'll put me in the gunnysack with a snake?"

"You got it girl! Now, tell Daddy you won't tell."

"I promise, Daddy, I won't tell."

Then HE bellowed out at me, "See this dead pine snake! See its stabbed head. How would you like your head stabbed with a pitchfork, just like it? That's what I would do to you if you ever told your Momma. Now, you won't ever tell, will you? You know, there are so many pine snakes here on Grandpa's farm I bet I could find a hundred of them. I could put them in the basement and lock you down there with them. I would do that if you ever told. Do you understand, Jackie?"

I nodded my head yes.

"Now, you wouldn't want that to happen, would you?"

"No!"

"Since it would be entirely your own fault, you wouldn't want to cause that to happen to yourself, would you?"

"No, Daddy."

"Do you understand, Jackie? Now, you won't ever tell, will you? Promise me you won't because I sure wouldn't want to have to lock you up in the basement with a bunch of slimy pine snakes or put you in a gunnysack with one of them."

"No, Daddy, I won't ever tell. I promise!"

HE started walking with the snake a little closer to me and then I blacked out.

The next thing I remember that day is stopping at McDonald's on the way home for a hamburger, french fries, and chocolate shake. As I numbly sat eating my food, I thought to myself, "*Somehow, some way, I will be someone -- someone very special. Just like I was on the tractor -- someone special. I can do it. I can. I know I can!*"

AN INNER CONVERSATION - Current Time

An angry voice in my head says, "Yeah, yeah, yeah, you'll be something special all right. A special little wimp that can't even take care of herself. You couldn't even protect yourself or your precious little 'Dolly' from HIM. Oh, yeah, that's right, you did protect The One Who Never Got Hurt. So what, so you protected a doll. Big deal."

"Thanks a lot Ms. Confidence!   We'd be out there on the end of the limb that you had pushed us to and you'd vanish. We'd be there standing out in the open, all by ourselves, feeling like a fool, not knowing what to say or do next."

"Well at least I got her to try things. If I hadn't given her confidence and encouragement, and pushed her some, where would she be now? She never would have driven that tractor so well. And where would you be Ms. Anger? You'd still be stuck down in my stomach; at least I encouraged you to come out and be sociable instead of being ignored all the time -- you can do it, you can, I know you can."

"Yeah, yeah, yeah, whatever."

"I did my best to give you and all of the others the confidence you needed to do your jobs the very best that you could, you all know that."

"While most all of the others wanted encouragement, there were a few who didn't seem to need or care for it. Regardless, I would always be there, issuing my words of confidence and encouragement.   They seemed to ignore me and go about their business, probably because The Angry One was there as well with her usual bitchiness, (Oh excuse me, Ms. Anger . . .) The Angry One was there as well with her usual admonishments. She wants me to refer to her in a more pleasant manner. My apologies!"

"The Angry One is right though. All too often, I would get

76

one of them excited about some project. She'd get right in there, go to work, and then I'd have to leave her there all alone because someone else was faltering. With the many-faceted spectrum of our psyche, I was constantly busy flitting from one part to another, and another, and then somewhere else. I was kept on constant alert, issuing confidence to whomever needed confidence at the moment they needed it the most. At least it got them up and on their own two feet, that was my job."

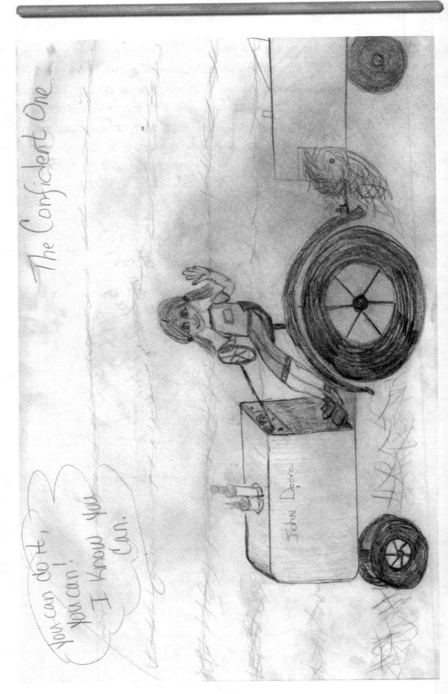

78

The Protector

So many words to tell,
so many feelings to share,
so many voices telling me to say nothing.
So much fear,
so much terror,
so much hurt,
so many voices telling me to say nothing.

Where do I go with what I have inside?
so many voices telling me to say nothing.
Say nothing,
say nothing,
Pretty soon, say nothing becomes nothing to say.
I have nothing to say.
I have nothing to say.
I am just dumb and stupid with nothing to say.
Maybe I'm pretty, maybe I'm smart,
but I am still just dumb and stupid with nothing to say.

Where do I go?
Oh, dear Lord, where do I go?
Even you don't hear me.
Nothing to say.
Nothing to say.
Run away,
go hide,
go quickly.
Nothing to say.
Nothing to say.

Hush and be still my child.
Feel my arms around you,
feel them warm you,
feel them calm you,
feel my fingers stroke through the hair on your head.
It is okay that you have nothing to say.
It is okay that you say nothing.

Hush and be still my child.
You are strong and have great courage.
You will find a way to say what you need to say.

Hush and be still my child.
No matter what HE or the world does or doesn't do,
you are safe from harm with me.
No one will hurt you here.
Guardian angels God will send thee all through this night.
Peace will attend thee all through this night.

Hush and be still my child.
Rock slowly with me,
breathe slowly,
breathe deeply,
calm yourself,
calm yourself.
Find the peace in your soul,
calm yourself.

There you go, that is so much better.
I feel your stillness,
I feel your calm.

Hush and be still my child.
Tomorrow's a brand new day.
The sun will shine.
You will find a way to say what you need to say.
You will say it better than anyone has ever said it before.
You will say it in a grand way and the world will hear you.
Yes, the whole world will hear your beautiful words.

Yes, you do know what to say.
You know what to say!
Your day will come.
You will find a way to say what you need to say.

Hush and be still my child.
Rock slowly with me,
breathe slowly,
breathe deeply,
calm yourself.

Possessing a limitless supply of courage
The Protector has been my guardian angel.
If any part of me becomes too distressed,
she takes over and those feelings soon disappear.
She restores order, balance, and harmony,
She gives me an inner peace.
A peace that reaches to the deepest depths of my body, mind, and soul.

She can be seen on my face
It is the look of strength
It is the look of determination
It is the look of an individual fighting to stay sane
in her extremely insane world.
She comforts

She soothes
She calms
She makes me feel safe
as she tells me,
Hush, and be still my child.

A Shopping Trip to Milwaukee

Later that same summer, my parents decided to take a road trip to Oregon to visit Ann and Doug, the mean babysitters. About two weeks before our trip, Momma said she needed to go shopping in Milwaukee to get some new clothing for all of us. Friday night we took Maria, who was just two years old, to Gramma Jameson's house and left from there early Saturday morning. Richard and I exuberantly jumped into the back seat of the car. We were so excited about our very first "big-city" shopping adventure.

To a six-year-old girl who had spent most of her few years on a very rural, very quiet country farm, the large department store seemed enormous. At first I held on really tight to Momma's hand. There were so many people moving around the store, and there seemed to be hundreds of tall clothing racks scattered as far as I could see in every direction. Momma suggested to HIM that HE and Richard go on their own way to the men's department to find their new clothes, and they made plans to meet in the sporting good's department at a specific time later in the day.

Momma began by sauntering around and around all of those racks, checking prices, holding shirts up to her face, asking me for my opinion on how the color looked on her, until she had an armload of things to try on. I patiently followed her back and forth from the clothing racks to the changing room and out to the mirrors as she tried on the variety of clothes she had selected. When Momma was satisfied that she had found an adequate abundance of new clothing for herself, she looked down at me and said, "Now, Jackie, it's your turn." She glanced around the floor we were on and realized there wasn't any children's clothing, so she found a clerk and said, "Can you tell us where we might find little girls' and toddler clothing?"

The nice clerk told Momma, "Well, that would be upstairs. If you go to the other side there," pointing in a direction behind us, "you can take the escalator up to the third floor and you'll find what you're looking for."

Momma said, "Thank you," to the clerk and proceeded in the direction the clerk had pointed to, with me in one hand and her packages in the other.

"Momma, what's an 'exkalater'?" I asked.

"Well, it is a staircase machine that takes you upstairs without you actually having to walk up the steps."

"Oh . . . how do you get on the machine, Momma?"

She chuckled a little and said, "We'll be there in just a minute, and I'll show you how we get on."

Although I was a little apprehensive at first, I quickly relaxed and began to enjoy riding the escalator. I asked Momma to go up and down a couple more times and she humored me until she decided we should continue our shopping. She picked out some shorts and tops, a pretty dress, pajamas, underwear and socks, and a new pair of shoes for me; and again, had me offer my opinions when she chose Maria's new clothing. After she had everything she wanted for her two daughters, she found HIM and Richard in the sporting goods department, nonchalantly relaxing in some lawn chairs by a tent display and talking about the camping supplies we'd need for our long trip west.

While they were all busy comparing tent features, I slowly tiptoed backwards, quietly sneaking away from them until I was around the corner and out of their sight. Then I scurried as fast as I could and headed straight to the escalators, hitching a ride on the up-going steps, I ascended into unknown territories. When I neared the top of the moving steps, I would squat down as long as I dared and watch each step mysteriously disappear into the floor, wondering where the steps went to, secretly wishing I could shrink and flatten out as thin as a piece of paper so I could follow them on their enigmatic journey beneath the store. Timing myself, I would stand up just in time to let my little feet ride off the step until the part I was standing on vanished under the floor and deposited me onto solid ground. I would zip around the banister in a flash to catch the next ride up. I imagined I was a flying horse riding up to the clouds, an angel riding up to heaven, and a pilot rocketing up to the moon -- it was better than the merry-go-round Momma had let me ride at the fair last summer.

Boarding the down-going escalator was a bit more tricky. I cautiously placed just one foot over the moving steps and held it there until I was bold enough to hop onto the capricious step at just the moment when one was projecting about three-quarters of the way out of the floor. Eventually I became more brave and even closed my eyes when I stepped out. I pictured myself in a cartoon, striding off the top of a high ledge, just like Wyle Coyote did when he got fooled by the Road Runner.

I rode all the way up the six flights of escalators and all the way down, at least a dozen times or more. What pulled me back to the present time and reality I'm not sure, but I suddenly realized I didn't know where my family was. Instead of continuing down the next escalator, I started looking around for them on the floor I was on. As I became more aware of the fact that they were not around and the realization sank in that I had lost them, I became frightened, and started to cry. Not knowing what to do, I decided to ride up to the next floor.

Approaching the top, I noticed a large black woman just standing there. Never having seen a person with black skin in all of my life, I didn't know what to think. I had heard about black people and saw some of them on TV, but I never imagined someone would have skin that dark. The next most noticeable thing about her, perhaps because I was coming up from below her, or perhaps because they were the most gigantic things I had ever seen, were her breasts. They started at her shoulders, extended at least a foot out from her body and ended somewhere near her waist. They took up the entire top portion of her body. After that, I saw that she had on a black dress with white polka dots, a wide-brimmed black hat with a white ribbon around the base of the top, and was holding onto a shiny black purse with her white-gloved hands. There were no nylons on her chubby dark legs, and she had on shiny black shoes. Her eyes were jet black in color and I watched them closely as I traveled to the top and stepped off the escalator. Because her eyes were so very dark, it was hard for me to see into them.

When she looked down at me smiling gently, I relaxed as she said, "Whasa madder, girl?"

"I can't find my Momma and my Daddy!"

"Oh, ya poor little thang. Come wid me and we'll find um fer ya. Okay?" She took me by the hand and the next thing I knew, I was back with my Momma who thanked the woman at least a dozen times for returning her little girl to her. Never having heard the way the black woman talked before, I asked my Momma why she talked funny.

"Well, Jackie, it would seem that she has a Southern accent. Perhaps she just recently moved here from down south somewhere or maybe she's visiting relatives. She sure was your guardian angel today, though, wasn't she?"

I replied, "Yes, Momma, I like that. She was my guardian angel today."

While my Momma was ecstatic to have me back, HE was mad and scolded me when Momma walked ahead with Richard. Holding up a rather large bag in HIS hand, HE shook it in my face, squeezed my arm roughly and said, "You see this bag here? Do you see it?"

"Yes, Daddy, I see it," I replied with a whimper.

"You know what's in this bag? Do you know? Answer me, girl!"

"No, Daddy, I don't know what's in it. You're hurting me. Please stop squeezing my arm so hard."

"I'll tell you what's in it. It is filled with snakes. I bought them at the pet store while your Momma and brother were looking all over tarnation for you. Now, if you go and run off again, I'll throw them at you as soon as I find you. They'll crawl all over you and bite you. You wouldn't want that to happen now, would you? Well, would you? Answer me, dammit, answer me now. Would you want me to throw these snakes in this bag at you?"

"No, Daddy!"

"Are you going to run away again?"

"No, Daddy!"

"Promise me you'll stay right by me for the rest of the day. Promise me, dammit!"

"I promise to stay right by you, Daddy. Please don't throw snakes at me."

By this time I was sobbing almost uncontrollably so HE stopped, wiped my nose and wiped my tears away with HIS handkerchief and said to me, "There now, you'll be fine. I just don't want you running off in this big store. You were lucky that nice lady brought you back to us today. Someone mean could have taken you away and done bad things to you. Now you stay real close. Okay? Smile for Daddy now. Okay?"

"Okay, Daddy. I'll stay close. I promise."

Not having finished shopping in the sporting goods department due to my disappearance, we returned there to get the other things everyone still needed. When we were done shopping and had something to eat, we piled all of our packages into the trunk of our car and headed home. After such a long day, I quickly fell asleep and had another bad dream.

We were back in the sporting goods department and I was still holding HIS hand. HE walked over to the counter, began talking to a clerk, and let go of me. Momma was over at the other side of the long L-shaped counter and I decided to walk over by her. I heard HIM laughing loudly behind me. HE called out my name. When I turned around to face HIM, HE had on those awful evil eyes, and HE tauntingly said, "Jackie, catch this!"

The bag that HE had told me was full of snakes went high, high

up in the air, almost to the ceiling, and started its descent toward me . .
. . All of sudden, instead of seeing the bag, I saw a beautiful
lady, The Protector, with her hand reaching out to me. The instant I
touched her hand I left my body and flew with her up to the ceiling
across from the counter. I watched the bag as it was coming down and
started screaming out, "No, don't catch that bag. Someone tell that
little girl down there (who was no longer me) that there are dangerous
snakes in that bag. No, little girl, don't touch it! Why doesn't anyone
hear me? ! Somebody, help! Please help her!" Just before the bag
was about to reach the little girl's outstretched hands, the lady who
had helped me earlier that day, grabbed the little girl and whisked her
away to safety.

The Chicago Zoo

Who would ever think that an eight-year-old girl's trip to a zoo would become one of the major pivotal events in her life; but it turned out to be that way for me. My parents had become good friends with a couple they had met when they all lived in Milwaukee. The couple had moved to Chicago a few years after Momma and HE moved north to Antigo, Wisconsin. They had kept in contact with each other over the years and visited each other from time to time. For a summer vacation, in what would have been the year I was eight years old, between second and third grade, my parents decided to go to Chicago to visit their friends and see some of the sites there. The most memorable part of the trip was our visit to the Field Museum of Natural History and the Chicago Zoo.

What kid could ever forget the excitement of walking into the Field Museum and seeing that first glimpse of the massive dinosaur skeleton that occupies nearly the entire length and height of the main foyer. And what a sense of wonder and mystery we had, along with a thousand questions that came to mind when we walked through the eerie strangeness of the Egyptian exhibit. There was the tomb of a pharaoh, which proudly boasted a black and golden head adornment with a hooded cobra at the very center of it. To give him sustenance and companionship on his journey to the afterlife, the Pharaoh had been given a wealth of golden objects. Coffins holding mummies of handmaidens and children were spooky to a young girl, and the curious pictures of ancient hieroglyphics on extraordinary pottery were baffling. We spent an entire day at the museum and were unable to see it in its entirety. It was truly an awe-inspiring place that sparked our imaginations, making them work overtime.

We all had an equal or greater excitement about going to the Chicago Zoo the very next day. It would be our first time to see real live African animals. Reality was much better than TV -- the elephants were larger, the giraffes were taller, and the lions louder than we ever could have imagined. The monkeys were comical and the rhinoceroses were fearsome. We were having a fun day until we got to the Herpetorium.

When we walked up to the building, I had no idea what a herpetorium was, but I heard Momma talking about snakes. I didn't want to go in and put up quite a fuss, but HE said, "Here, Jackie, take my hand and stay close by me. I'll make sure you are safe. The snakes are all in glass cages and can't get out anyway." Uncomfortable and uncertain about what would be inside, I took HIS hand. Once inside, my heart instantly started racing wildly with panic because of the darkness as our eyes took a few seconds to adjust from the bright sunlight outside to the darkened exhibit area inside. All around the outside of the room and in a square on the inside of the room were small and large glass cages with every conceivable kind of snake -- pythons, boa constrictors, anacondas, green and black mambas, rattlesnakes, copperheads. All were very colorful, some were rather small, others were very large. Some of them were lying completely motionless as if they were sleeping or in a trance. Others nonchalantly slithered about in their cages in search of food or something to do. None of them seemed to have any concern that hundreds of people were walking by looking at them all day long. None of them that is, except the King Cobra.

The cobra's cage was set apart from the others. It was raised off the floor about two feet and continued all the way to the ceiling. By far, it was one of the largest cages in the room. There was a sign on the glass that said, "Please, do not tap on glass." The King Cobra happened to be very active and was moving quickly about the cage looking out, as if it were agitated at the crowd passing by. HE stopped at the cage and was amused by watching the busy creature.

I said, "Daddy, let's go. I don't like this snake building. It scares me."

HE didn't respond. When HE began tapping on the glass, the King Cobra responded by raising up its head, so HE continued to tap.

"Daddy, I don't like this. It is scaring me, and I want to go now!" I pulled on HIS hand to free mine, but HE wouldn't let go of me. I nervously glanced about the room and noticed that my mother and brother were behind us on the other side of the room near the place where some people were leaving through the door under the exit sign. We were almost alone in the room. Then HE looked down at me with HIS wicked-evil-driven eyes and sheepish grin on HIS lips.

HE said, "Jackie, watch the snake and see what it does."

When I looked back at the glass cage, my eyes opened wide and my body was instantly filled with terror. The huge snake was directly in front of me. There on the other side of the glass was its malicious head setting atop its two hooded eyes. It flicked its tongue and moved closer toward the glass and the sound of HIS tapping. It was so close, only a few inches from me. The only thing separating me from certain doom was the thin piece of glass.

I was absolutely terrified, unable to move, unable to scream, watching its every movement. I wanted to scream for Momma, I wanted to run, I wanted to hide, I wanted to cry out in terror, I wanted to escape, but I could not make my body do anything.

The snake climbed higher and higher, moving its hooded head back and forth, trying to see beyond the glass, responding to the continuous tapping noise HE was making, until it was even with HIS tapping hand. I remained involuntarily motionless as I watched the formidable reptile that had me so powerfully mesmerized.

HE continued to tap on the glass and HE continued to smile wickedly. Then, Momma broke the spell HE had on the snake and me.

She said, "Wiley, stop tapping on that glass. Besides, we're leaving now," as she walked through the exit door.

Holding me close to HIM, HE hissed as HE jerked my whole arm and I jumped back. HE grabbed me tighter, knelt down before me, looked me square in the eyes with that wild, driven glare of HIS, whispered to me, "Jackie, if you ever tell your mother about our little 'secret,' I'll come back here and get this snake and lock you in a room with it! Do you understand? You don't want that to happen to you, do you?" Still unable to get any words to come out of my mouth, I barely managed to move my hypnotized self to ever so slightly nod my head in agreement. HE shook me again, harder this time and said, "Do you understand, Jackie? I'll get this snake if you ever say anything! Speak to me, girl, do you understand? We're not leaving this building until you answer me." HE shook me again, demanding an oral answer.

With the softest of voices, which was all I could squeak out, I said, "Yes, Daddy, I understand. I will never tell. I promise! I promise!" All I knew at that moment is that I wanted to be out of that building, back into the sunlight, and back to Momma. We left then, and I remember nothing else about the rest of the day at the zoo or about the rest of the trip.

I had no idea at the time what a huge moment that had been in my life and how far-reaching the affects were to be. HE had me right where HE wanted me -- a little girl utterly silenced and perfectly terrified of the big man and the big snake. From that moment on, HIS ability to use me however HE wanted and to keep me silent about it was complete. My determination to escape was rendered powerless and I quickly surrendered to HIM whenever HE reminded me of the big snake, or any snake for that matter.

6 The Ugly One

Sometimes when I look at myself in the mirror
I look deep into my eyes and wonder,
who are you in there?

Then I see torment, ugly torment, in my eyes.
So much ugly torment that I have to turn away.
I can't stand to look at me so how can the world?

It feels like I was unfairly accused,
It feels as if I am an outsider,
unwanted,
rejected,
by everyone.

It feels like there is something wrong with me,
something that is not wrong with anyone else.
Something so wrong,
that the world cannot stand to look at me
because
I am so ugly.

I see torment, ugly torment, in my eyes.

I May be Ugly, But I am not A Witch

Some big and some small, some bumpy and some smooth, some with small black dots on top of large cauliflower-headed warts. Lots of ugly warts. Warts infested almost every knuckle joint of both hands, all over the inside of my palms, and thirty or so little ones grew on my right wrist. They were so ugly. Picking at them made them hurt and bleed, but sometimes I picked them all of the way off anyway and they still grew back bigger and uglier than before.

During recess one afternoon, another girl and I were playing together when she noticed all of the warts on my hands and wrist. Immediately, she sprang back, pointed a finger at me, and started screaming at the top of her lungs, "You have hundreds of big ugly warts on your hands. You must be a witch!" She dashed over to the other girls we had been playing with and pointed her finger at me again, exclaiming to them, "Jackie is a witch. She has huge ugly warts all over her hands and there must be a hundred of them on the inside of her wrist!"

Then they all chimed in, "Jackie has ugly warts. She must be a witch! Jackie has ugly warts. She must be a witch! We don't play with witches. Get away from us!" Then they went around the playground telling all of the other kids, chanting together and pointing their fingers at me. "Jackie is an ugly witch with ugly warts. We don't play with witches. Stay away from us!"

As I stood there in shock and shame, I looked down at my ugly warts. *Where did they all come from and why do I have so many of them? I never should have picked up all those toads -- Momma said they'd give me warts. I am so ugly.*

"I am not a witch!" I cried out in my defense. "I am not a witch -- I just have some ugly warts!"

They kept on pointing their fingers at me and chanted again, "Jackie is an ugly witch with ugly warts."

97

I was standing near the corner of the school building so I turned away from them and stood with my face in the corner. The hot, wet tears showered down my face as if there were a thunderstorm letting loose its cloudburst inside my eyes. I cried out inside myself, *I am not a witch!, I am not a witch! I know how ugly I am, but I am not a witch!*

When the bell rang to go inside, I still stood sobbing in the corner which just happened to be near the stairs we used to enter the building. As the other kids walked by my ugly body, they chanted to me again. "Jackie is an ugly witch with ugly warts -- we don't play with witches!" I did not look at any of them as they passed behind me. When everyone else had gone in, I wiped the tears and snot off on the inside of my shirt, straightened up my shoulders, and told myself, *I definitely am not a witch, I am just very ugly.*

Back in class one of them drew a picture of an ugly witch with a big wart on her nose and passed the note to me, pointed her finger, and said quietly, "Ugly witch, ugly warts. We won't play with an ugly witch!" Out on the playground, the chanting and finger pointing went on for a week or more, and they never played with me again.

Now ostracized from my former group of friends, I kept to myself until I made a new friend. Diane was a girl in our class who had an abnormality that caused her head to be much larger than normal. The kids called her "space alien" or "watermelon head." Several times she had to have surgery to take some of the water out to relieve the pressure on her brain, and she'd come back to school with no hair on her head whatsoever because it had all been shaved off. When that happened, the kids, unrelenting in their laughter and teasing, ignominiously dubbed her the official "Bald Space Alien Watermelon Head" of New Holstein Elementary School.

She knew she was not an alien, nor a watermelon head, and I knew I wasn't a witch; but I knew how ugly I was. My new friend and I were able to find consolation in each other. We erected invisible boundaries around ourselves to shield us against the undeserving, deliberate verbal cruelties and outright rejection of our peers. Once inside the contrived mental fortress in our own corner of the playground, we didn't care what the rest of the class thought of us. Their words became meaningless and their rejection was nullified.

She was a beautiful person, my new friend, Diane. I will forever be grateful for her unconditional acceptance of me and for being able to see beyond the ugly warts and my ugly persona. My warts eventually went away. I do not know if her condition was every corrected or cured, I hope so.

They think I'm ugly
I'm not a witch
It's not true
But, I know
I'm ugly
Jackie has hundreds of warts all over her hands and wrists. She must be an ugly witch. Tell everyone not to play with her!
The Ugly One

7 The Pretender

The Pretender took us to the fantasy world of
Musical-make-believe-you-are-whatever-you-want-to-be Land.
We mostly wanted to be safe, so
We were safe in our
Musical-make-believe-you-are-whatever-you-want-to-be Land.

She would give us our escape and our adventure
She would give us our romance and our love
She would give us our salvation and our peace.
We were safe in our Musical-make-believe-you-are-whatever-you-
want-to-be Land.

We could be different, we could be powerful, We could be big
We could be the beautiful dame comin' 'round a
pretty snow-capped mountain driving six white horses.
We could be a flittering butterfly if we wanted.
We were safe in our
Musical-make-believe-you-are-whatever-you-want-to-be Land.

HE was never, never, ever there.
We were safe in our
Musical-make-believe-you-are-whatever-you-want-to-be Land.

The Piano

Her name was Jennifer; she was a new girl in our class and she sat down by me at lunch on her first day. By far, she was the most beautiful girl in our school. She was shorter than I was and had a small body. A person would expect to see at least some timidness in her face, being brand new to our school and all. Instead, her eyes, being the most remarkable color of green I had ever seen, twinkled with merriment, inviting you to linger with her, to discover more about her, and to want to be near her. Glistening, shiny hair adorned her head; it was very long, dark brown in color with a reddish tint to it when the light hit it just right. I could just imagine her Momma standing for hours the previous night rag-wrapping every piece to perfection to get all of those long curls to bounce flawlessly when she moved. Also, she must have had to get up very early in the morning to unwrap and comb each piece, laying it gently in place. All those curls were pulled back with a beautiful sateen pink headband with short puffy bangs fanning out evenly over her creamy-colored forehead, and her long curled hair fell forward over the headband just enough to delicately frame her exquisite face. Her dress had to be one of the most beautiful dresses I had ever seen. The entire dress had a satin pink underlay that appeared everywhere underneath the sheer lacy white top layer. The plain round neckline was decorated with a pink satin edging. At the fitted waistline, there was a three-inch satin pink sash that matched the underlay and was tied into a large bow at the back of the dress. The skirt of the dress burst out into a thousand lacy folds that went all the way around this beautiful girl Jennifer. Her pure white socks had been cuffed over and were encircled by a delicate, white frilly-lace edging with a tiny little pink bow resting on the outside of each leg just above her ankles. On her dainty little feet were the shiniest black shoes I had ever seen, and from her hand dangled an elegant silver chain-link handle that was attached to a black purse which was just as shiny as her shoes. I thought that her parents must be absolutely wonderful and obviously very rich. Certain that her life was charmed in every way, I immediately wanted to live her life instead of mine.

As we talked and got to know each other a little over lunch, I learned that she played the piano. She chatted on about taking piano lessons, practicing all the time, and how she enjoyed it a lot. That was it! I could learn how to play the piano and then I could be just like the beautiful girl Jennifer. I had a mission now, all I had to do was convince Momma to let me take lessons.

"Please, Momma, please. I just have to learn how to play the piano!" I pled with Momma for weeks, it seemed.

"Well, Jackie," she would say, "lessons cost money, a lot of money and what if you don't like it? Besides, we don't even have a piano for you to play on."

"Momma, I don't need a piano, I just need lessons. Let me take lessons for awhile and see how it goes. You don't have to buy me a piano, just let me take the lessons. Please, Momma, please. I really want to do this!" Finally, through my persistence, I won! She arranged lessons for me with a lady that was a few blocks from school. Every Tuesday right after lunch I would walk to her house for my lesson and then go back in time for afternoon classes. My first books were so exciting with all of the strange black lines and dots with stems and flags. It was a wonderful dream come true.

Now, how was I going to do this without a piano? The first few lessons were easy, just learning what notes on the pages matched the keys on the piano keyboard. There was a picture of a keyboard right in the music book so I could use that to practice. But after a few weeks, I was actually starting to play some music and I had to come up with a plan. I had it! I'd draw a keyboard on our wood floor; each slat of wood would be a key of the piano. I went right to work on the floor in my bedroom and drew an entire keyboard with the black keys colored in. It worked just fine and I could even hear the music in my head as I practiced on my wooden-floor piano.

After about three months of paying for weekly piano lessons, my Momma decided she had better call the piano teacher to see how I was doing. She didn't want to be throwing her hard-earned money away uselessly.

"Oh, Jackie is doing wonderfully. What!! She has no piano? Well, then she is doing just great."

My Momma was excited for me when I came home and she described her conversation with the piano teacher. She said, "Jackie, I guess we're going to have to find you a piano now!"

"Thank you, Momma. Thank you, Momma. You have no idea how much this means to me. Thank you, Momma." I jumped up and down and ran around the rooms of the house like I was bouncing on a pogo stick gleefully yelling, "I'm getting a piano! I'm getting a piano! Thank you, Momma. Thank you, Momma. I'm getting a piano!"

After the initial conversation my Momma had with my piano teacher about not having a piano, I was a little embarrassed about it and I didn't want her to think I hadn't been practicing. Of course, she asked me about it at my next lesson. "You are playing so well for not having a piano at home, you certainly must be practicing somewhere. Where do you practice?"

Too ashamed to admit I was playing on the floor of my bedroom, I quickly made up a lie.

"Well, I go over to our neighbor's house and play there."

"Oh, really," she exclaimed.

Actually, I had never been in the neighbor's house, but I had heard piano playing coming out of the windows.

"What is your neighbor's name?" I told her the name and she replied, "Oh, Mrs. Prichard! She is a dear friend of mine and goes to my church. I'll have to talk to her about you on Sunday when I see her."

Oh, boy, I thought, now she's going to find out about me. I didn't say anything more in hopes that she wouldn't bring it up again, but at my very next lesson she did bring it up again.

As soon as I sat down on the piano bench and got out my lesson for the week, she said, "You know, Jackie, I talked to Mrs. Prichard on Sunday, and she claims she didn't have a clue what I was talking about. She said she certainly didn't have any little girl coming to her house to practice on her piano! You lied to me, didn't you?"

"Well . . . er . . . yes, I did, I am very sorry."

"Why did you do that, Jackie?"

"Well . . . ah . . . I was just so embarrassed that I didn't have a piano."

"Your mother told me that, so where have you been practicing?"

"Well . . . um . . . I practice in my bedroom on the floor. I drew the entire piano keyboard, using each narrow slat of wood for one white key and I colored in the black keys."

She said, "That's amazing, Jackie. You mustn't be ashamed of that. You should be proud of yourself. You have done extremely well for just having practiced on the floor. Imagine what you could do with a real piano."

I told her how Momma said we were going to buy a piano now, how excited I was about it, and then we went on with my lesson.

Unfortunately, finding a used piano took some time. We watched the musical instrument for sale section of the paper every day looking for a used piano and nothing, nothing, nothing. We bought the weekend papers and still nothing. Then, one day, there it was. A used, dark-brown console Spinet piano in perfect condition, only $50.00, too! We called right away even though it was a long distance call to Sheboygan. We said we would come right away and buy it. We jumped in the car and started the one hour or so drive to Sheboygan. HE got lost a little and had trouble finding the street the lady lived on.

When we finally got there, the lady apologized and said, "Someone just came and bought it. I am so sorry, I couldn't wait for you. I had to sell it and they were here first. You understand how it is."

I ran back to the car and threw myself in the back seat, crying uncontrollably, "I'm never going to get a piano."

Momma tried to comfort me on the way home and assured me that we would keep looking until we eventually found one.

"Whatever we find, Momma, it won't be as nice as this one. It won't be as nice!" In a couple of weeks we bought an old upright piano that was not quite in tune for $35.00. I didn't really care and I knew it wasn't as nice as the one we missed in Sheboygan, but it was still a piano and I was happy.

As the lessons continued and I became able to play more melodies, I pretended to be the beautiful girl Jennifer. We would be at an elegant ball when we played "Lavender and Lace." A most handsome prince would waltz us around a gleaming marble floor beneath shimmering crystal chandeliers while all of the onlookers marveled at our beauty and grace as we danced so merrily. I would go on an "African Safari" and hear all of the sounds of the animals while I drove around in a Jeep wearing my chic khaki outfit and straw hat wrapped with a leopard scarf. Or, I could be lying on the ground looking up at the "Idyll Autumn Leaf" as it danced and floated effortlessly on its long journey down to earth from its high oak branch whence it came. "Skating at the Park," in a beautiful winter suit made of red wool with fluffy black edging at the wrists and neck, I would be the envy of all who watched me skate like an Olympic gold medalist. I would twirl around, perform perfect figure eights, jump high, land ever so lightly, and go into a magnificent spin to finish my outstanding routine. Then the audience would offer me their applause for what seemed to be an effortless and flawless performance.

The beautiful girl Jennifer and I could venture anywhere our music took us. We could be anyone, we could be everyone, we could be no one at all, but we were someone special, the beautiful girl Jennifer and I.

109

8 The Truthful One

I promise to tell the truth,
the whole truth,
HIS truth,
and nothing but the truth,
so help me God!

HE said, "LIE"
Momma said, "Tell the truth."

HE said,
"Tell lies and lie so good that
it not only sounds like the truth,
but that it becomes the truth."

Momma said,
"Tell the truth,
always tell the truth,
and the world will respect you for it."

HE said, "LIE"
Momma said, "Tell the truth."

HE said,
"She must never know the truth
because if she does,
she'll hate you and leave you,
and it will be all your fault."

Momma said,
"The Bible teaches the Truth shall set you free."

HE said,
"The truth will make you an enemy,
an outcast,
no one will love you anymore."

Momma said,
"Don't be afraid of the truth,
the truth is your friend,
it is your character that is at stake.
If you lie,
people won't like you,
they won't trust you.
You must always tell the truth."

HE said, "LIE"
Momma said, "Tell the truth."

I promise to tell the truth,
the whole truth,
HIS truth,
and nothing but the truth,
so help me God!

I Promise to Tell the Truth, So Help Me God!

Her purse was on the kitchen counter and I was craving a chocolate candy bar. *If I took only five cents I could buy a chocolate bar down at the corner grocery store. I bet she'd never even miss it. Where is she right now? Uhm, hanging out the laundry. She'll be there awhile. I'll quickly open her purse, find her wallet without disturbing anything else, take out a nickel, close the wallet, and put it back in her purse. Such an easy thing to do. She'll never know I took her money. Heck, it's only one coin. Okay, go for it now while she's outside. Gee, she has a lot of coins in here. Maybe I should take a little more -- that way I could buy something else tomorrow and maybe even a soda pop. Yep, I'm taking thirty-five cents, she'll never even miss it.* Then, I ran out the back door and told Momma I was going for a walk.

She smiled and said, "Don't go too far. See you later, Sweetheart."

On my way home I dawdled along especially slow in order to have the whole chocolate bar gone before I got back. My favorite way to eat a chocolate bar was to break off one small chunk at a time and let it melt awhile on my tongue. Then I would use my tongue to press it to the roof of my mouth and rub my tongue all over it very slowly so that I could savor every molecule of the chocolate flavor for as long as possible until it melted completely away. I hated the part when I was forced to let the flavor go because I had swallowed it all. It was so smooth and creamy on my tongue, it tasted so good, and the best thing about it was that I had enough money left over to buy another one tomorrow and the next day too, with money still left over for something else. *This was so great, why didn't I think about getting money from her wallet before? Maybe when this money is all gone, I'll take some more. A little here, a little bit there, she'll never even miss it.*

As I skipped up to the house, I noticed the bread truck

pulling out into the alley away from our house. Back in those days, we had a bread man, a milk man, a Fuller Brush man, and an ice cream man. They all came by the house once or twice a week to deliver the goods that we had ordered on their previous visit. Momma was standing in the kitchen with her purse in one hand and was rummaging through the bottom of it with her other hand; her empty wallet sat wide open on the kitchen counter and there were several rows of coins neatly arranged by like denomination. She looked at me inquisitively and I thought, *Uh oh, I think I might be in trouble.*

She said, "Jackie, your father gave me change this morning before HE left for work to buy bread from the bread man. Funny thing is, when I went to get it from my wallet, I was missing exactly thirty-five cents. You wouldn't happen to know anything about that, would you?"

I immediately replied, "No, Momma."

The only thing is though, Momma and I were the only ones home that day. She hadn't taken the money, she knew she had put that money in her wallet, and she knew I had gone off pretty slick and happy. She picked me up, set me on the counter and piercingly stared directly into my eyes.

"Jackie," she said as she squeezed my arms and shook me gently, "I put that money in my wallet and now it is gone! You were the only one in the house. Now tell me the truth, did you or did you not take that money?"

I turned away in shame and laughed a little, I could not look directly into her eyes.

She squeezed my arms harder, lightly shook me again and said, "Jackie, look me in the eyes and tell me if you did or did not take that money!"

I started crying and knew I had been caught. No use lying to her, she knew the truth anyway. "Yes, Momma, I took the money. I'm sorry. I'll never do it again, I promise! I'll never do it again, I'm sorry! I have some of it left, here it is!" I quickly reached into my pocket, grabbed the coins, and handed her the twenty-five cents I was going use for future candy purchases. Well my bottom became sore as she spanked me a good one, my eyes became reddened as she scorned me, and my heart became saddened as she sent me to my room for the rest of that beautiful summer afternoon.

Lying on my bed and feeling sorry for my current situation, I realized it wasn't missing the rest of the beautiful summer afternoon that saddened me the most, nor was it the fact that I wouldn't have that money for another candy bar or two, I was sad because I had made Momma so furious with me. My thoughts turned to all of the things HE had told me and I was suddenly afraid she would leave me because I had been such a naughty girl. From now on, I promised myself, *I will never steal from her again and will always tell her the truth about everything, except, of course, HIS secret. I promise to tell the truth, the whole truth, HIS "truth" and nothing but the truth, so help me God! Momma will love me -- she will see that I am a good girl and will never leave me.*

Keeping the Secret in the Victims' Circle

As long as it was a little person that HE could easily intimidate, HE was indiscriminate about whom HE "bothered." We all knew about HIS secret because we were all HIS victims -- we talked to each other about it, we would hear it happening to one of us in another room, and sometimes HE would tell us about experiences with one of the others.

The depth of my intense passion of not wanting anyone else to know went far, far beyond extreme. Not telling was of paramount importance to me, I resolutely believed my very existence depended on it. So, I became a self-appointed, "do-not-tell" teacher in the interest of self-preservation at about ten years of age and began instructing the other girls (my younger sister, Maria, and my Aunt Margaret, who was two years younger than I) in the finer points of not telling.

Blabber-mouth Maria was forever talking nonsense about anything and everything. She simply would not shut up. We would jokingly bribe her with money if she would just be quiet for five minutes. *Definitely a vulnerability in that girl, undisciplined in quietness and hot-headed sometimes, I had to constantly remind her never to tell.*

For one school year when my Aunt Margaret was about eight years old, she and her mother (my maternal grandmother) moved to the upstairs apartment above our house in the city. My grandmother worked in the factory during the school year to earn some extra income and would go back to the farm on the weekends. Unfortunately this move made Margaret easily accessible to HIM. While she knew how to be quiet, she was very unstable emotionally. Her mom and dad were ancient; they were grandparents more than once already, and they simply seemed incapable of meeting her needs on a daily basis. I watched her as she would throw herself into fits of anger, jumping up and down, screaming at her parents that they didn't care anything about her, that they didn't know what she wanted from them, and that they never would understand her. Unable to understand her myself, her anger scared me, and I wondered how could she be so out of control. *Another possible vulnerability here, completely unpredictable in her wild fits of anger, she needed so much love and attention, both of which she didn't get from either of her parents. I decided I must constantly remind her as well about how important it was to never tell about HIM, even if she was really angry.*

"Now, Margaret and Maria, let's review what I just told you. Why do we never, never tell anyone what HE did?"

We would recite HIS lies, we would make up our own lies, we would role-play situations where someone was asking us about HIM and drill each other, practicing the lies with great precision. I would recapitulate for them the horrible things that HE had taught me about what would happen if we ever told on HIM. We went over it again and again, until I was confident that they knew how to lie very well and they knew why they had to lie very well.

I decided that if I could ensure that they never told anyone, I would greatly improve my chances of always having a mother, of avoiding horrible snake pits, and having life in me until I grew old. Nearing puberty, I took on a new, and perhaps, an even greater burden -- that of shame. What HE did felt dirty, it felt sick. I was completely embarrassed of HIM, I was totally ashamed of myself, and according to HIM, it was all my fault. I certainly, definitely, positively, indubitably didn't want anyone outside of our victims' circle to find out about my shameful secret.

9 The Runner

She never talked to anyone else.
She did not know anyone else.
She just ran as fast as she could.

She did one thing and only one thing, she ran.

The Angry One would chastise and berate her
in an attempt to admonish her to run faster.
The Confident One would tell her how fast she was,
how good she was, and how she could go much faster.

The Runner paid no attention to the idle chiding
going on in her head.

She did one thing and only one thing, she ran.

She was a loner.
She needed no one flinging anger at her.
She needed no one flinging encouragement at her.
She needed nothing, nor did she wish for anything.
She just needed to run.

She did one thing and only one thing, she ran.

We would often speculate about what made Grandpa Jameson so ornery. He seemed to be the most grouchy and complaining person on Earth. If there were anything to grumble about, he would. We could not conceive how one person could find so many subjects to whine and gripe over in one day. He would crab at Gramma, he would crab at Margaret, he would crab at anyone in the house -- how come this, how come that, crab, crab, crab. He would condemn Mother Nature and the weather, fret over the cows, fume endlessly about the nonsense of going into space, the government and paying taxes, cuss at any religion, or denounce the hegemonies that set the price of milk. And, if the children did anything that irritated him, well, then it was time to hound Jackie because it was all her fault.

In spite of Grampa, Richard, Maria and I were always excited to go to the farm and visit Aunt Margaret, who was much more like a sister to us than an aunt. The farm was over-abundantly teeming with an endless apportionment of invigorating and fun diversions, new-fashioned realms to explore in even diminutive shifts in the seasons, and unknown marvels to discover in the seemingly mundane, coupled with lots of time on our hands, young imaginations, and no fear. It was a young person's oasis. For some reason it seemed like the universe stopped for us when we were at the farm. It was an extraordinary world where minutes lasted for hours and days lasted for eons as we filled each second with illusions of grandeur that only a child's mind could divine and, more importantly, we were free. Free to be whatever and whomever we wanted to be, free to envision possibilities, free to dream of our futures, and free to wish we never had to go back home.

Up in the barn, there was a heavy rope tied from the highest rafter that hung over the hayloft that was perfect for one of our

123

favorite things to do. Grabbing onto the rope by the big knot tied at the bottom of it, we would climb up a wooden ladder, which was nailed to the middle of the wall at the far end of the barn until we reached a ten-inch-wide support beam that spanned the entire width of the barn. Carelessly stepping out onto the beam, we would make our way across it until we were able to get onto the top of the adjacent granary, which was quite a bit higher than the hay below. Once there, we would pull the rope as far back into the corner as possible, quickly calculating just the right amount of rope we'd need to soar through mid-air effortlessly -- enough to reach from our hands and arms outstretched above our heads down to our feet. When we were all psyched up and with the rope in hand, we'd take off running as fast as we could to build up as much speed as possible before we reached the edge of the granary. At exactly the same moment as the granary disappeared from underneath our feet, we would grab on tight with both hands, place our feet on the big knot, and feel the rush of the thick and humid barn air as we swung swiftly over the hay. We would let go of the rope when we had flown back and forth several times and at just the opportune moment to fall comfortably into the soft hay landing net which we had created by tearing apart several bales of hay. This was done very gracefully as we sang and pretended to be the daring young kids on the flying trapeze.

We also pretended to be tightrope walkers as we bravely walked across the huge, ten-inch center beams, which stretched across the entire width of the barn and hung about twelve feet above the barn floor. Of course, that wasn't too risky considering that the hay bales were neatly stacked just inches below the beams. Beam-walking was at its best, however, after the hay had been used up as feed for the cows. That is when we truly became fearless young beam walkers. We would cheer for each other as we boldly walked across the beam without even flinching or giving any thought to the idea that we could have fallen off and collided with the hard floor.

The small river that meandered through Grampa's farm was another great place for kids to play. In the summer we'd swim, walk the logs that lay across the river, and then when we got bored doing that we would walk the outside of the bridge. It was the perfect size for a kid; we'd hang onto the top steel I-beam of the bridge with our hands hooked all the way over the edge. Our tiptoes fit just comfortably on the bottom ledge of the rusty, orange steel bridge which was separated about every two feet by vertical supports. We'd have to lift our tiptoes off the beam and swing one foot at a time around to the other side of the vertical beams. Back and forth we would go on the outside of the bridge -- all forty feet of it -- pretending to be heroic spies on a secret mission to save the world. Down under us about seven feet, the shallow river rippled and gurgled as it felt its way through the haphazard maze of boulders. When the sun and water flirted with each other on top of the large rocks, we pretended they were talking to us in a secret code, using intricate patterns of glittering quartz to try to deceive us.

Then Grandpa would come along and POOF, the magical adventure we were experiencing would quickly scatter away along with the twinkles from our eyes as he discovered what we were up to and begin griping about it.

"Jackie! Get those kids off that bridge. How many times do I have to tell you not to play on that damn thing. I might as well be talking to the dumb pigeons up on top of the barn! Haven't you got a single lick of common sense in your head? What is the matter with you?"

On and on he would go, rattling off an entire list of accusations, hurling insults at me, and almost always delivering one of his harsh spankings to my bottom side. "You are the oldest and you should know better. Where is your sense of responsibility – don't you know these kids could get hurt up there?"

Usually, I would bow my head in true shame, but wonder

why he just picked on me. *Why didn't he ever say anything to the other kids? Sure, I'm older than Margaret and Maria, but Richard is older than I am and he was up there too. Why doesn't he ever yell at him? It isn't just my fault. It isn't fair. He should yell at all of us and not just me.* I did not understand.

The summer when I was ten years old, there was a family reunion at Grandpa Jameson's farm. Everyone was there: the entire family with every single one of my cousins, all of the aunts and uncles and all of their husbands or wives. Doug and Ann had come back from Oregon for the first time since they had left and the rest of the family came from all over Wisconsin. What were twelve kids going to do while the grownups got reacquainted? Well those of us who were the more frequent fliers had to show the newcomers how much fun we could have up in the hayloft. So off we went and showed them "the ropes." If flying on the rope was fun with four kids, it was a blast with twelve. Of course, we had to show off for them too. Each one of us took turns carefully describing and demonstrating the special skills and techniques that we had personally developed to get the most exhilaration out of our flights across the top of the hay. When they all got the hang of it, we decided to give ourselves a name, "The Crazy Cousins Flying Troupe." My cousin, Bonnie, who was two years older than I, was chosen as the Master of Ceremonies. As each person would step atop the granary, take hold of the rope, and prepare for his or her flight, she would announce their name and give a detailed accounting of what technique that person was about to attempt, give a drum roll . . . and then . . . Grandpa walked into the barn.

"Jackie! Get down here right this instant."

Everyone looked around puzzled at each other wondering why he called my name, although I was already well used to it. And then, there in front of everyone, he totally disgraced me with his barrage of insults. "Jackie, you should know better than to take these kids up into the hay."

126

I thought to myself, *it wasn't my idea, it was Richard and Emily that suggested we go up there.* I tried to interject, "But Grandpa, it . . . ."

"Now you are the oldest one, Jackie. How many times do I have to tell you to stay out of there? You must have rocks for brains or be as stupid as that idiot straw man out in my garden!"

"But Grandpa, I'm not the old. . . ."

"Just shut up and listen to me. You had better get those kids out of the hay and do it right now."

"Come on you guys, we gotta get out of the barn," I poignantly called up to them to come down out of the hay. I started to cry in shame and in anger as Grandpa harshly grabbed my arm, turned me around over his knee, and proceeded to whip my bottom side harder than usual.

"Now, you get down to the house and sit by your mother before you get into any more trouble."

As I dejectedly walked alone down to the house, I mulled over what had just taken place. *I wasn't the oldest. There were three kids there older than I was, I just happened to be the tallest. How could he call me an idiot and spank me in front of everyone? It isn't fair, it just isn't fair. It wasn't even my idea to go up there in the first place. Why doesn't he blame the right people and why does he always just pick on me? I could not make the words come out, but I wanted to turn around and scream at him, but I knew that would be disrespectful to my elder, and besides, I didn't want another spanking.* I went and sat down next to Momma just as I was told to do. HE was there too. A few minutes later, Grandpa came storming into the house, pointed his finger at me and Momma, and began to yell at us in front of all the grownups.

He said, "Mary and Wiley, that girl of yours had all of those kids up in the hayloft tearing my bales of hay all to hell. You better make sure she doesn't drag them up there again. Do you understand?"

128

HE decided to do something about it right away. HE stood up, took HIS belt off, doubled it in half and proceeded to beat me with it right there in the living room. It had been bad enough that Grandpa had affronted me while all of the cousins looked on, now HE heightened my feelings of degradation and humiliation by whipping me in front of all my aunts and uncles too.

Awhile later that same day, HE began giving all the kids a ride on a little motor scooter. One at a time HE would take them up the hill on the lonely country gravel road in front of Grampa's farm and drive out of sight. One at a time HE would bring them back smiling and laughing, having a good time. When HE came back I raised my hand and yelled, "Me, Daddy! Me, Daddy! Choose me, Please!" HE would call out the name of the next kid, but it wasn't me so my excitement sank. Over and over again HE would come back. Over and over again HE would choose someone else until HE had given all eleven of them a ride. Finally, there was no one else left to ride but me.

HE called my name and said, "Jump on my most special, oldest and most beautiful girl. Hang on tight now. Let's go!"

With all the waiting, anticipation, and disappointment, I was thrilled for my turn. Up the hill we zoomed, my hair was blown backwards as the hot, summer wind raced past us and stirred-up gravel dust settled in my mouth leaving it a little dry. I hung on tight around HIS waist just like HE said. The scooter's narrow back tire slipped slightly out to the side over the loose gravel as HE revved up the engine to make it up to the top of the steep hill. I hung on a little tighter. It felt like we were flying as we whizzed past the fields in the bright sunlight. Then we carelessly dipped through areas of dappling shade fashioned by the tall trees that lined the road on either side. The overhanging branches were stretching down, as if making an attempt to reach out to us. I recklessly let go of HIM to raise my hand to touch them as we sped by and they laughed with me as they mockingly slapped me back with their leafy fingers. The forest was filled with many tints and shades of green that all blurred together on either side of the quiet road. It was a great ride and I was experiencing everything that I had envisioned when I was impatiently awaiting my turn.

We began to slow down at Newton Lake Road -- I thought to turn around and head back to the farm. When HE didn't turn around and continued down the secluded road, I started to get scared right away. The road that ran in front of Grandpa's farm was lonely enough, but Newton Lake Road was lonelier yet. I knew there would be nobody down there.

"Why are we going down here, Daddy?" I hollered over the noisy hum of the little motor scooter.

He replied, "Oh, just to look at the lake for awhile."

I knew better. I knew exactly what HE had in mind. Instant fear, instant anger. *Why were you so extremely stupid not see HIS scheme to get you alone?*

The Runner started forming her plan while we drove along the lake road that twisted and wound up and down and around little hills all the way down to the lake. As soon as the scooter was just about to stop, I would push myself backwards to jump off the seat and start running back toward the main road. I would run fast. I would run faster and harder than I had ever run before. I would fly, just as if I were flying over the hay. All I had to do was run fast enough to get around a corner where HE couldn't see me. Then, I would trick HIM by turning off the road and running even faster to get as deep as possible into the woods as quickly as possible. I would keep running all the way back to the farm. HE wouldn't catch me today. No way.

Okay, HE is slowing the scooter down. Get ready, get ready . . . . Now, Push! Jump! Run! Run . . . Run . . . .

Go faster, faster.

No, you idiot! Don't waste time looking back over your shoulder, just keep running away.

Come on Jackie , get going! You've got to make it to the top of the hill and around the corner. I don't care if the muscles in your legs are burning, aching, throbbing. Do you hear those footsteps? HE's catching up, HE's catching up!

You call yourself a runner? You've got to be kidding. You're a pathetic excuse for a human being. Get going, move it! Move those lazy, no good legs of yours. Faster, faster or HE'll catch you! Run! Run! R . . . .

Fear, fright, panic, dismay as HE grabbed my arm. I kicked, I screamed, I bit, I broke loose, I ran again. What seemed like a ten-mile run was probably only about two hundred yards up a little hill until I felt HIS vile, forceful hand on my arm again. Now out of breath and hope, I knew I wasn't fast enough. HE dragged me off into the woods. HE stilled my flailing arms and legs. HE grabbed at my clothing. Sinking spirit, despair, overpowered. I was little, HE was big.

The overhanging branches were stretching down, as if making an attempt to reach out to us. I recklessly let go of HIM to raise my hand to touch them as we sped by and they laughed with me as they mockingly slapped me back with their leafy fingers. The forest was filled with many tints and shades of green that all blurred together on either side of the quiet road. It was a great ride and I was experiencing everything that I had envisioned when I was impatiently awaiting my turn, and more. Sometimes, even running as fast as a zooming motor scooter wasn't fast enough.

Run Run Run
Run Run Faster Up
Faster Giving
He's Catching
Run

The Runner

Jacqueline

With so many visitors at the farm, finding a sleeping place for everyone was a challenge -- the adults got the beds in the big house and the kids got to sleep on the floor in the "little house." There was a little house on the farm that resembled a small trailer home, although it wasn't a trailer at all. Even though it was modestly furnished with the basic necessities of any home, no one lived in it, and I have no idea what its purpose was, it was just there. We were never allowed to play in it, so the fact that they were going to let us sleep over there, let alone by ourselves, was a real miracle as well as a dream come true. We would be away from the adults in our own house and we could do whatever we wanted all night long.

After our moms made beds out of blankets for all of the girls on the little house's living room floor and got the three boys settled in the tiny bedroom at the back, they gave us a flashlight and left. Yippee! We're alone at last! The full moon shone brightly through the big picture window that covered most of the wall at one end of the living room. It created so much light, that we didn't even need the flashlight to see. My cousin, Bonnie, was a great storyteller. She had us gather around her and form a tight circle. She told us funny stories, sad stories, and ghost stories. When she told the ghost stories, we passed the flashlight around to each other and held it under our chins to make spooky shadows on our faces. We listened, laughed, and got scared. Then, we had a rambunctious pillow fight with the boys until we got tired of that. We ended up making a play out of one of Bonnie's funniest stories and then decided we would perform for the adults the next afternoon. Parts were assigned to everyone and we practiced our lines and movements. Carefully, I watched Bonnie as she directed the other kids. She spoke clearly, she shared her knowledge with an easy confidence, and she laughed wholeheartedly as we stumbled through our parts. In the moonlight she shone and I quietly wished I could be like her instead of the stupid-idiot, quiet, tongue-tied, dumbbell I was. Well, as with any group of kids, all night long didn't last all night. Eventually, we became tired and succumbed to the sleep that was beckoning all of us after our long, busy day.

Later in the night, I was awakened by the sound of the door opening and two female voices whispering in the dark. As they came closer to us, I realized the voices belonged to Gramma and Ann, the mean babysitter. They were checking on us so I pretended to be asleep, lying motionless with my eyes closed.

I heard Gramma say, "Well, it looks like they are all sound asleep." Then, she continued, "You know, Ann, I feel so sorry for her mother, Mary, because Jackie is such a lazy girl. She doesn't help with anything and Mary has to do everything herself. Jackie just wants to play, play, play all the time and never lifts a finger around the house. I don't understand how a girl can be so inconsiderate. You know she doesn't mind her mother either. She is simply no good for nothing and the sorriest excuse for a daughter I've ever seen in all my life. She'll never amount to anything that one. I feel so sorry for Mary." They went to the tiny bedroom to check on the boys and then left the little house.

Oh, my heart ached. This had been a very, very bad day. First Grandpa had wrongly accused me, then HE "bothered" me, and now this. Hot, wet tears came gushing out of my eyes. *No*, I said to myself, *it just isn't true. They don't know me, they don't know that I do the dishes every single night after supper and make my bed and clean up the bathroom when I'm done. It isn't true what she said. I am not inconsiderate. I love my mother, I mind my mother, I do what she says. Why would Gramma tell lies about me? I am good for something, I am. It isn't true. I am a good girl. I do the best I can, I do. I am only a ten-year-old girl. What do they expect of me? They are just as bad as Grandpa, always yelling at me when it's the other kids that start things. Why do they hate me so much?* As more and more tears poured out of me, I wiped them away on the sheets. *Why do they pick on me? I will amount to something. I will amount to a lot. They don't know what I am capable of. I will show them. I will show all of them how good I am. Eventually, they will have to admit that I did amount to something and they will have to eat their words when they see the truth.*

The agony of the entire day swelled in my head, mangled at my soul, and poured out of my eyes for what seemed like hours until finally, sleep came and rescued me from my misery.

136

An Entire Family of "Botherers"

Perhaps it was my new set of developing breasts that caused him to notice me that day in a different way than before, or maybe his nineteen-year-old hormones were acting up. Who knows why something like this happens. Uncle Alan, HIS brother, had been away to college for the past year and had just arrived home for the summer. This was the first time he had seen me since he had left last fall. I remember him being so excited to smell the fresh country air, to hear crickets and birds instead of all the noisy traffic he had left behind in the big city, and to see the stars in the night sky that weren't visible where he had attended school.

He held his hands high over his head upward toward heaven and declared, "I love the country! Hooray for country! I am so glad to be home." His jubilance was catching, and soon we were all dancing, singing, and leaping around like silly frogs in the grass.

Later, several of us decided to play hide-and-go-seek in the barn. When the person that was "it" started counting down, Alan took me by the hand and said, "Come on, Jackie, you can hide with me. Where should we hide? Let's see . . . ." Looking around us he decided quickly, "Come on, we'll go up in the hayloft." When we got to the ladder, he said to me, "Ladies first," as he bent at the waist with one arm across his waist and the other in a swinging motion like that of a noble prince.

"Why thank you, Sir Alan," I replied and did a curtsy before proceeding up the steps.

When we both were up in the hayloft, we looked around for a good hiding spot and got settled in to wait.

He said to me, "Come here, Jackie, and sit on my lap. Let me look at you. My, how you have grown up to be such a pretty, young lady. How old are you now anyway?"

I told him, "I just turned twelve. It was my golden birthday this year -- twelve on the twelfth."

One of his arms was around my back holding me up as I sat on his knee and with the other hand he caught a strand of hair that had fallen out of my ponytail and tucked it gently behind my ear.

"You look much older than that, you know. In fact, see what you did to me sitting on my lap?"

In one swift movement of his free hand, he had unzipped his pants and pulled "it" out. He grabbed me tightly with the hand he had behind my back and wouldn't let me go when I began struggling with him.

"Alan, you're scaring me. Let me go!"

He replied, "Come on, Jackie, I just want you to touch it. That's all. I am not going to hurt you. It would just feel so good if you would touch it." With his free hand he grabbed my right hand and placed it on his private thing. He continued, "There, you see, that isn't so bad. You touch me and I'll touch you. You'll see how nice it feels and you will like it, you really will." I didn't want to touch him and I didn't like the notion of him touching me at all, so I pulled my hand away, and then to my relief, we heard someone coming.

"Quick, Jackie, get up. I have to zip up my pants. Now don't you tell anyone what we did up here today. They will think you are a very bad girl if you do and you will get in a lot of trouble. Promise me you won't tell. Okay? Okay? You wouldn't want to get in trouble, would you?"

With shame hanging over me, I weakly said, "No."

He hurried to zip up and said, "Well, don't tell anyone then! Come on now. We have to run back so we don't get caught."

Alan was going to college to become a minister and I didn't understand why or how someone in that position could have done something like that. I just knew it was wrong and it felt awful. But I was not going to tell anyone about it because I didn't want to get in trouble.

After we were done playing Hide 'n Go Seek, three of us,

my Aunt Cheri, HIS youngest sister, and HIS seventeen-year-old brother, Uncle Gary, and I, went upstairs and were just hangin' out on Cheri's bed. Uncle Gary reminded me of "Hoss" from the *Bonanza* series -- he was the heftier one of all the uncles, very tall, and naturally good-humored. Although he was slightly quieter than his older brother, Alan, he had lots of goofy things to say and could always make me laugh.

Gary had ordered a tiny camera from a magazine and had just received it a few days before. It was about two inches wide, one-and-a-half inches high, and supposedly capable of taking real, bona fide pictures. He told me it was a secret spy camera that allowed him to take "special" pictures.

"I can take pictures of people with their clothes on and when they are developed, the people are completely naked! The people will never know what I did, and I will have an entire collection of naked pictures to look at. I figure I am going to take it to school and take pictures of all the girls with the biggest tits."

"Gary!" I said, "You can't do that. And besides, there is no such thing. Let me see that camera!"

He immediately began taking pictures of Cheri and me, so we quickly put one of our arms across our breast area and the other one down below and crossed our legs. "I'm going to have naked pictures of both of you girls." Click, click, click went the tiny camera.

"I don't believe you! So take all the pictures you want. Now, let me see that camera." He handed it to me, I examined it, and I wanted one for myself; it was such a neat little thing. I asked, "Does this camera actually take real pictures?"

"Of course it does, silly girl, but you're right. It doesn't take naked pictures. I was just joshing with you."

We began to hit him with the pillows from the bed, "We knew it all the time!"

Later in the evening on that same day, we arrived at this

139

field of tall grass and brush, which wasn't owned by either of my grandfathers and I no longer recall the purpose for our being there. Quite a few of us went and we all piled out of two cars, which had been parked by the entrance gate to the field. The gate was swung open and we all proceeded into the field. HE was there too, talking to a man that met us there and deciding what was going to happen next. Along the entire north end of the field, about one-quarter of a mile away and spanning in either direction, there was a long ridge of hills that was covered with a forest of trees. On the south end of the field there was a fence-line running along the road as far as you could see. An agreement was reached and then everyone that was with us took off to do whatever we were there to do.

Uncle Gary hadn't started off with the others and called to me, "Jackie, come back here for a minute." So I walked back to where he was leaning against a fence-post. "Why don't you and I stay here instead of going along. I feel lazy and don't want to walk all that way."

"Okay," I replied, "I guess I could hang out here and keep you company."

For a long while we talked idly about nothing and then out of the blue, he told me a dirty sex joke.

"Uncle Gary!" I said, "I'm just a little girl, you shouldn't tell me a joke like that!"

"Well, Jackie," he continued, "you don't look like such a little girl. In fact, you are starting to look all grown up with those two nice tits of yours, and I would really like to see them!"

I swiftly moved my arms across my chest in an attempt to hide my breasts and in a truly shocked, surprised tone I said, "Gary, you shouldn't be talking like that or looking at my tits. After all, I am your niece."

"Oh, Jackie, don't be so surprised; it happens all the time. Relatives are always attracted to each other, it's a fact of life."

"I don't think so, Gary."

"Well it's true, Jackie."

Then he unzipped his pants and pulled the big thing out of them and let it just hang there and said to me, "Look what you have gone and made me do with those tits of yours. See, I am attracted to you. I would like you to rub it for awhile. It would feel so good."

"I don't want to touch it or rub it, Gary. It is disgusting!" I turned away to walk back to the car and he grabbed me by the arm.

"Come on, Jackie, just touch it for a minute. It would feel so good to me and make me so happy. Come on. It won't bite you or hurt you. Just touch it for me. Please." He took my hand and placed it on himself. With his other hand, he slipped down my pants and started to feel me. It was such an awful feeling and I hated it. I didn't want to touch him, and I certainly didn't want him touching me; but he held me there and made my hand move up and down on his thing while he wiggled his fingers that were in my panties.

This only went on for about one minute and then we heard voices. He quickly pulled his hand out of my pants and began zipping his pants back up. He said very sharply to me, "Jackie, you mustn't tell anyone what we were doing. If you do, they will think you are a very, very bad girl. Now, don't tell. Promise me you won't tell. You don't want anyone thinking you are a bad girl, do you? Do you?"

"No, I won't tell," I once again said with shame in my mind.

When the others got back, we piled back into the cars and began driving back to the house. I was thinking to myself as we drove along. *What is with this family? Do all of them "bother" girls?*

SECTION III:

THE JUNIOR HIGH YEARS

As difficult as the Junior High years are for a young person, they were doubly difficult for me. I was very tall, taller than most of the boys in my eighth grade class. My nicknames were "Moose," "Klutz," or "Ditz." HE continued to assault me and began telling me bizarre things about young men.

10 The Religious One

When the nightmares wake us
in the deep, dark night,
there is only one remedy
Jesus and prayer.

I call upon Jesus, God, and the Holy Spirit.
I pray fervently
I pray swiftly
I pray without pausing.

I pray to purge my mind of the evil that has invaded it.
I throw Jesus in the evil's face,
 it struggles with me and resists leaving.
Finally, the evil can't take it anymore and vanishes away.
Jesus and I win again.

My prayers reach up toward heaven and
heaven reaches down towards me.
I am wrapped warmly in its arms as it comforts and quiets me.
When only Jesus remains with His visions of heaven,
I relax and begin to allow myself to feel sleepy.
As I continue my prayers, my breathing slows
my heart stops pounding and untroubled sleep returns.
Thanks be to Jesus and prayer.

When the nightmares wake us
in the deep, dark night,
there is only one remedy
Jesus and prayer.

A Basement Full of Snakes

Having worked in the electrical motor manufacturing factory for about five-and-a-half years, HE decided HE had had enough factory work and began looking for some other type of employment. On a Sunday afternoon HE was perusing the <u>Milwaukee Journal</u> want ads and there HE found it -- a perfect opportunity for HIM. It was a concrete business venture for sale over in the Wausau area. HE exclaimed to Momma, "Gee, Mary, I could be my own boss and you could be my bookkeeper and secretary. We could form our own corporation and we wouldn't have anyone standing over our shoulders telling us how to do things or when to go to work. Hey, you could stay home with the kids and quit this craziness of working all night. What do you think, Honey?"

She was very skeptical, "You know, we would be giving up a guaranteed, good income. In that business you wouldn't have a weekly paycheck and neither would I if I stayed home. Could we afford to give up two paychecks and insurance? What about medical bills? How would we pay them? And what would we do in the winter for money? You couldn't pour basements in the winter months? I don't know, Wiley, it sounds very risky to me."

Convincing and suave as HE was, HE persuaded her to go check it out. The next weekend they drove to Wausau to talk to the man selling the business. When they came home, they had decided to buy the business and we would be moving to Wausau in the summer after we sold our house. It all happened so fast. The house was sold on June 17, 1964, and we had packed up and moved to Wausau by the end of the month. They had rented an older, but rather large, two-story house and planned to stay there until the business started to pick up and they would have more money coming in. The move went smoothly and suddenly. We were in a new house again.

With Momma not working nights anymore, I was not as easily accessible to HIM as I was before. Nevertheless, I am not saying that HE quit assaulting me or that the assaults were less frequent. Every time that HE and I were alone, usually because of a carefully planned scheme devised by HIM, HE would "bother" me.

Going someplace alone with HIM in the car became risky, and once I learned this trick of HIS, I made up excuses as to why I couldn't accompany HIM. Sometimes, however, HE manipulated me into going with HIM under some sort of false pretense. And there I was, caught off guard again, alone in the car with HIM in harm's way. Another of HIS tricks that I watched closely for was when HE would send Momma somewhere to get something. If she was gone to the store for just a few minutes, HE would see her absence as a free license to assault me again.

The first Saturday after we had moved into our rented house, Momma decided to go shopping for some things that she needed. My Aunt Margaret, who was visiting for the weekend, and Maria went with her. HE was gone at the time, so I decided to stay home to watch TV. A little while later, HE walked into the living room and asked where my mother had gone. After I told HIM, I noticed that evil look in HIS eyes that I had learned to interpret so well. HE went into the bathroom and I fled upstairs.

All of a sudden I was frantic, desperate, vulnerable, terrified, and driven to hide. I needed to hide as quickly and quietly as possible so HE wouldn't find me. A good hiding place meant HE wouldn't be "bothering" me this time.

There was a very large walk-in, cedar-lined closet, crammed full of out-of-season stuff, like warm blankets, hunting clothes, sporting gear, and old winter coats -- all kinds of large-sized things that a little kid could hide in, under, or behind. There were some large boxes left over from our recent move into that house and Momma's old cedar chest that I could fit into. I climbed into the cedar chest that had some winter clothing in it to lie on, closed the lid, and waited quietly. HE didn't find me and went away. I felt fortunate that day because all too often there was no place to hide, except in my mind. I decided I should stay in the closet until Momma got home and before I knew it, I had fallen asleep.

Later that morning, Maria and Aunt Margaret came looking for me. I woke up when I heard them calling me and walked sleepily out of the closet. They wondered what I was doing in there, so I just said I was looking for something, sat down for awhile, and must have fallen asleep.

We lived in that rented house for about one year when my parents decided to build a new house. I was entering seventh grade and was twelve years old. In order to avoid paying rent while the house was being completed over the summer, we moved into the new basement, which HE had carefully made HIMSELF.

It was about the same time we moved into the basement that we started going to a new Baptist church that had just been established nearby. Since it was a brand-new church, the membership was small and the young, new pastor needed lots of help. It wasn't long before we were all quite involved in church activities. We went early to Sunday School classes, we started to pray before meals, and the Pastor and his wife came over to visit us in our basement home. Because I knew how to play the piano, I was asked to play hymns for Sunday School convocation. After church on Sunday, the Pastor would give me a list of hymns they were going to sing the following week and I would practice them for hours, singing along as I did. Momma bought me a Bible to study, which I read faithfully every night before going to sleep. The small Baptist church quickly became a major dynamism in my life that consumed much of my time, energy, and more importantly, became an escape from HIM.

Each Sunday at the end of Pastor John's sermon, he would invite those in attendance to come to pray at the altar. Pastor John's weekly invitation was almost always the same. He'd say, "Repent and be saved. Give your heart to Jesus. Ask Him to come into your soul and cleanse you with the Blood of the Lamb. Just as you are, that's how Jesus takes you. Just as you are, He will take your pitiful life, remold it, remove the ugliness of sin, and make you new again. You will be reborn into the beauty of His light and His love. Turn away from the world and give your heart to Jesus, the King of Kings, the Lord of Lords, the Savior that gave His life so that you may live eternally with God in heaven above. Don't hesitate one second longer, come and pray to Jesus, ask Him to cleanse you of your sins. Ask Him to come into your heart. Ask Him to change you forever. Ask Him to reign supreme in your life. Come, my children, and kneel before the altar of God. Give yourself to Him before it is too late. Before damnation comes to you. Amen, Lord Jesus, a precious child of God has come to accept you as her savior. Praise be to God. And another young man comes. May these young souls be blessed by God, Himself. Praise God. Amen. Amen. Another soul comes. Praise be to God. The Lord is working here today. Do you feel it? Do you feel the Holy Spirit among you? He is calling each and every one of you to His service. Praise be to Jesus! We need some help up here. Will some mature, born-again Christians come and pray with these young people that have come to the altar to give their hearts to Jesus on this holy day. Amen. Thank you, Brother. Thank you, Sister. Thank you. Bless your soul. Pray with these young people who want to give their hearts and souls to Jesus. Amen. Amen. Praise be to God for his work here today!"

Eight of us accepted Jesus as our Savior that day. Pastor John gently put his hand on each person's shoulder as he started at the far end of the line of newly born-again Christians and slowly worked his way down toward me. He said to each one, "Ella, what did you do here today? Christine? Dave? Larry?"

Each one shyly responded, "I asked Jesus into my heart to forgive my sins!"

After each one answered, Pastor John laid his hand on top of each head and prayed, "Thank you Lord Jesus for this beautiful young person that has asked you to cleanse his/her heart from all unrighteousness and has asked you to forgive him/her. We pray that you will bless and keep this soul safe from harm and close to your side in the warmth of your love. Praise be to God! Amen! Amen!"

When he got to me, he said, "Jackie, What have you done here today?" While tears streamed down my cheeks, too afraid to speak, he said, "What have you done here today child? Don't be afraid to speak up for the Lord."

Quietly whispering just to him, I said, "I asked Jesus to come into my heart and he wants me to be a missionary!"

Pastor John's face lit up and he exclaimed, "Praise be to God! This child has been called by the Lord God Almighty to be a missionary. Praise God! Praise God! Great blessings are among us today. Amen! Amen! What a day the Lord has made for us today. So many blessings, so many young people asking God to come into their hearts and forgive them of their sins. Let's all sing praises of God's amazing grace."

Since the Lord had so graciously blessed Pastor John with a called missionary, literally thrown down at his feet, he felt the need to put this missionary to work immediately.

"You know, Jackie, there is no need to wait until after you graduate from college to start your service as a missionary. You can begin serving the Lord right now, right here at Our Savior Baptist Church, even if you are only thirteen years old! As a new church in this area, there are so many things that need to be done, so many souls that need to be saved, and so many leaders needed to do it all. The Lord can use you, Jackie, right here in your own home town. I believe He has great things in store for you."

My work as a missionary began -- Sunday School teacher, Vacation Bible School teacher, pianist for worship services, youth group leader, summer missionary program, summer Bible camp, door-to-door canvasser, church secretary, and more. Pastor John was always there to encourage me, to laugh with me, to give me guidance, and to give me more to do. In a major way, all the church work was my salvation through my tormented teen years. An added bonus, in a way, was that no one from my school attended this church. There was no one that knew the real truth about me, that I was shy, ugly, and dumb. This is it, I thought to myself, a place for me to fit in, a place for me to be someone special, a place for me to be loved. It gave me the forgiveness I felt I needed, a direction to follow, a belief in a better life to come, and a reason to continue living this one.

When we finally moved upstairs in our brand new home, the vacated basement looked empty and so large. It was also much cooler down there in the hot summertime than it was upstairs, so Maria and I played down there quite often. We drew hopscotch squares on the floor, rode our bicycles around and around, and played house with her little tea set. There was one recurrent nightmare about that basement that I had dreamt dozens of times.

In the dream we were home alone. HE told me to go down into the basement because HE had a nice surprise for me down there. HE told me to walk over to the far end of the basement and stand with my face toward the wall until HE let me know when HIS big surprise was all ready for me. (I hoped HE had bought the roller skates that Maria and I had asked for. We thought it would be fun to roller skate on the new concrete basement floor.) I heard another voice behind me, but I didn't recognize it.

HE said, "Don't look now until I tell you to." I was getting excited and the anticipation was almost more than I could bear. I heard packages rattling around a little bit, and finally, HE said, "Okay, Jackie, you can turn around now."

When I turned around, my eyes went to the laughter I heard. I saw HIM with someone I didn't know sitting on the steps all the way across the room. When I noticed some movement out of the corner of my eyes and looked down at the floor, I nearly fainted and began screaming. All over the basement floor were snakes of every size. Large ones, small ones, different colors, some slithering around, some flicking out their tongues, others coiled up, and many of them headed my way.

"Oh my God, oh my God, help me! Help me! Get me out of here. Help Me! Please, help me!"

They just sat on the steps and laughed at me as I screamed louder and louder.

"Jackie, be careful. Don't let the snakes bite you."

There were many other such nightmares that recurred frequently. Writhing, slimy, twisting, filthy, rising up aggressively, fangs gnashing, tortuously hissing, masses of fiendish snakes, all coming at me. The devil, himself, along with his horde of dark and evil demons completely surround me, nudge me, beguilingly cajole me to follow them as they tauntingly lead me to the edge of an extremely deep ravine which is harboring a raging river of flaming, dancing, spewing hot lava. Sinister, persistent, terrifyingly hideous, blood-thirsty murderers with long, shining, razor-edged knives chasing me into a dark, dead-end corner. Running, running, running, but going no where.

Picking up the largest of the snakes, I am quickly overpowered. As the thing turns toward my face, its huge mouth and fangs begin coming down on my head; demons begin pushing me over the edge of the ravine; the murderers place their knives on the skin above my heart or to my throat -- thundering heartbeat, paralyzed body -- unable to move, paralyzed voice -- unable to scream. Consciousness comes at the very last nanosecond prior to my certain untimely and horrific death. Breathing is rapid and my heart is beating so fast and so hard that it would fling itself to the moon and back if it were a boomerang. The mind is racing fiercely out of control. Even though consciousness has come to me, the nightmare has not ended. The visions are still swarming around the room, darting in and out at me, still trying to seize control of me. I close my eyes, but hastily open them again because the visions are far worse in my mind. Hot, salty tears of fear gush out, pouring down my cheeks like an avalanche advancing down the mountainside at a thousand miles an hour.

God, help me!

My Father who art in heaven, hallowed be Thy name. Thy kingdom come, Thy will be done on earth as it is in heaven. Lead us not into temptation, but deliver us from EVIL. For thine is the kingdom, and the power and the glory, for ever and ever. Amen.

Jesus, Jesus, Jesus. What a wonderful name. Jesus, Jesus, Jesus all heaven and earth proclaim. Kings and kingdoms may all pass away, but there's something about that name. I command you, Satan, in the name of Jesus Christ my Savior, depart from me. I hold up his cross in your face. You can't stand to look at it, can you?

Satan laughs, "Ha, Ha, Ha," and says to me, "You give me all that religious shit. It means nothing to me. Who are you trying to kid? You call yourself a Christian? What do you ever do for God? What has He ever done for you? Why does God let HIM do what HE does to you? Do you think God loves you? If He loved you, don't you think He would stop HIM? Don't you think He would save you? No, He just lets you keep getting hurt over and over and over again. What kind of God would do that? He's pathetic if you ask me. Now, if you listened to me, on the other hand, ..."

I reply, Stop! You cannot claim me or harm me. Get out of here Satan! Jesus, Jesus, Jesus. You can't stand his name, can you? Jesus, Jesus, Jesus. For God so loved the world that He gave His only begotten Son that whosoever believeth in him shall not perish, but have everlasting life. Go away, leave me alone. Jesus, Jesus, Jesus. I believe in Jesus Christ the Son of God. I believe that

Jesus washed my sins away. I believe that I will stand at the throne of God one day and claim Jesus Christ as my Lord and Savior. God will put his hand on my hand and lead me through the gates of heaven. Go away, leave me. Jesus, Jesus, Jesus. I believe that God loves me. Jesus, Jesus, Jesus. This is my Father's world, and to my listening ears, all nature sings and round me rings, the music of the spheres. Jesus, Jesus, Jesus. I have a song that Jesus gave me. It was sent from heaven above. There never was a sweeter melody. It's the melody of love. In my heart there rings a melody, there rings a melody of love. Jesus, Jesus, Jesus. Just as I am without one plea, but that Thy blood was shed for me. And that Thou bidst me come to Thee, o Lamb of God, I come, I come. Jesus, Jesus, Jesus. Amazing grace, how sweet the sound that saved a wretch like me. I once was lost, but now am found, was blind, but now I see. Jesus, Jesus, Jesus. Sweet hour of prayer, sweet hour of prayer, that calls me from a world of care and bids me at my Father's throne, make all my wants and wishes known. In seasons of distress and grief my soul has often found relief and oft escaped the tempter's snare. By thy return, sweet hour of prayer. Jesus, Jesus, Jesus. Holy Spirit my heart yearns for Thee. Holy Spirit abide in me. Make me clean; oh, make me pure. I must know the double cure. Holy Spirit be my Guide. Holy Spirit, be Thou mine. Jesus, Jesus, Jesus. When peace like a river attendeth my way. When sorrows like sea billows flow. Whatever my lot, Thou hast taught me to say, it is well, it is well, with my soul. It is well, it is well, with my soul! Amen, Amen, Amen. Thank you, Lord Jesus, for giving me comfort. Thank you, Lord Jesus, for giving me strength.

Prayer became my only remedy to annihilate the fear and even the faintest vestiges of the chronic nightmares that plague me to this day.

11 THE ANGRY ONE

No anger.
Mustn't let anger show,
much too dangerous.

Anger turn inward
we are safer that way,
just stay down there.

No tears,
hide it, run from it,
do anything with it,
but don't let anger show on the outside,
just stay down there.

Down anger, back where you belong.
Back down
into the pit of my stomach.
Tear up my stomach if you want,
just stay down there.

Yell and scream at me all you want,
but stay down there.
Call me any name you want,
just stay down there.

Yell at the world
silently
all you want,
just stay down there.

Stomach problems, doctor treatments,
no questions asked, no comments given,
no one must know,
no one must hear,
no one must wonder.

You will never get to
The One Who Never Got Hurt,
we will protect her from you.
We have to protect her from you
and you don't need to know why,
just stay down there.

No matter what anyone does to you,
just stay down there.
You cannot scream out loud,
just stay down there.
You cannot show the world,
just stay down there.

You cannot feel, you cannot have
a voice,
you cannot
BE,
just stay down there.

No anger.
Mustn't let anger show,
much too dangerous.

No anger.

Stomach Trouble

"Momma, Momma, wake up." I gently rocked her shoulder in the middle of the night.

"Jackie, what is it? What time is it?" Momma asked sleepily.

"Momma, my stomach and back hurts so bad that I can't sleep, and I can't stand the pain anymore. What should I do?" I moaned. Momma got up, put her arm around my shoulder to lead me into the kitchen and turned the light on. She lightly gasped when she turned around and saw me holding my stomach with both arms, bent over in pain, with tears on my cheeks and an anguished look all over my face.

"Oh, my! You are in pain, you poor thing. Where does it hurt, Jackie?"

As I rubbed my belly, I said, "It hurts all over here, through the center of my stomach, it feels like it's burning up inside, as if my guts are on fire. My back hurts really bad, too, and I ache all over."

Momma tenderly felt my forehead and said, "It feels like you have a fever and sounds like you have a bad case of indigestion. I'll give you some aspirin for the fever and something to coat your stomach. Maybe that will help." She went to the bathroom and hurriedly came back with two aspirins and a pink bottle. Pouring some of the pink liquid into a large spoon, she said, "Here, Jackie, drink this . . . and another spoonful . . . there you go." Handing me a glass of water she said, "Now, take these aspirins and hopefully, that will help you feel better."

"I hope so, Momma."

"Now let's get you back to bed and we'll see how you are feeling in the morning." She walked me to my bedroom, pulled the covers over me, and sat down on the bed next to me. Affectionately brushing my hair back away from my face with her hand, she quietly hummed a soothing melody. After a while, she said, "Did the medicine help a little yet?"

"I think so, Momma."

"Well, if you are not feeling better in the morning, we'll take you to the doctor to see if there is anything he can do for you. Okay?"

"Okay. Thank you, Momma."

"Try to get some rest now." Momma leaned over and gave me a light kiss on my forehead. "Good night, sweetheart."

"Good night, Momma." I tossed and turned, but finally went to sleep.

When I got up in the morning, there was still an excruciating pain in my stomach and back. Momma called school to say I wouldn't be there and then called the doctor for an appointment. The doctor said I had a fever, there was evidence of infection in my urine, and he thought I might have a kidney infection. He wasn't sure about my stomach ache, but decided he wanted to put me in the hospital for some more tests.

I ended up staying in the hospital for three days and had an upper GI series, kidney-function tests, x-rays, and an entire host of other probing and prodding tests. My fever came down with the antibiotics they had given me for the kidney infection. They also found that I had severe gastritis, which was an inflammation of my stomach lining, and gave me medicine for that along with a list of foods I should avoid for awhile. When I was released from the hospital, Momma was instructed to keep me quiet and restful, and then take me to the doctor's office in one week for a checkup.

Having missed almost two weeks of school and having been so sick, Momma decided to buy me a new outfit for my return to school. She brought home a pretty, white blouse that had the new long-pointed collar style, a long, dark-brown, six-gore skirt, and a nubby, white and brown, v-neck sweater that buttoned in front. She had also bought me a new white slip, brown shoes, and nylons. It was one of the nicest outfits I felt I had gotten in a long time.

The school nurse needed to see me on my first day back. She commented on how sick I must have been and said how pretty I looked. I shyly told her about the new clothing Momma had bought for me. I did feel proud, very pretty, and somehow, I felt very special since so many people had taken such good care me.

A Footnote from the Voices Within

We know this is The Angry One's story, but we need to tell Anger's story from our point of view for you to understand why we did what we did to her.

Anger observed in others always seemed to be equated with being out of control. Since we were not about to let an emotion be our ruin, we could not allow Anger to be in control of us. Being out of control was an unacceptable risk No Anger meant we would not be spurting out "the secret" in the middle of an out-of-control moment. Anger, therefore, was always gagged.

As soon as we felt her rising up in our throat, she was instantaneously squelched. The throat was tightened, the muscles were flexed, and the mounting tensions were almost effortlessly subdued. We were so good at repressing Anger that it seemed we were like an expertly-trained attack team swiftly defeating our enemy as we sentenced her back to our center to be imprisoned there.

When HE had us cornered and we had to turn away from the violation of our body, we let go of our restraints on Anger. The festering rage was let loose as Anger rose out of our mouth and surged through our being. The fury she felt in her internal prison was precisely unleashed on HIM as she fought for herself. She would fight ferociously until there was no strength left in her, until she was overcome with pain, or even until unbridled, unyielding Anger could no longer challenge the consequences of the all-

consuming fear HE was able to evoke. When Anger was beaten, she ashamedly retreated back down to our center, poignantly returning on her own volition to her lonely exiled existence.

Because she was unable to succeed in defeating HIM physically and we would not let her defeat HIM verbally, Anger had nowhere to go outside of her internal confinement, so she incessantly rebuked us from our center. Unlike some, Anger was aware of all of the voices -- she knew each one of us intimately. She knew our strengths, she knew our weaknesses, and she knew exactly where, when, and how to strike to make us feel totally inadequate, completely insignificant, and all together contemptible.

Due to Anger's unrelenting bombardment of self-inflicted condemnations, we never let Anger get to The One Who Never Got Hurt. Tragically and ironically, Anger was scary to us, Anger harmed us, and Anger could have saved us.

The Angry One's Inner Dialogue

You are all just a bunch of wimps! Jesus, Jesus, Jesus! Help Me! Cry your eyes out, you stupid ninny and be afraid of the dark. So you have nightmares. Deal with it. They're just stupid dreams. And who is "The One Who Never Got Hurt"? Let's tell the stupid little bitch and get it over with. Why should she be so "protected" all the time? I hate her. The rest of us are suffering, so why shouldn't she? So you want me to shut up? Why should I? You've all had your chance to talk, so why shouldn't I?

You're all just a bunch of losers anyway. The Hider thinks she did her job so well. Okay then, why did HE find me almost <u>all</u> the time? And The Runner? She couldn't run if her life depended on it. HE always caught me, didn't HE? Oh yeah, I know she held a track record. Big deal! It never helped me out when I needed it to. Who is she trying to kid anyway? The only reason she won that record is because nobody else wanted to run that distance.

And where were the rest of you? Hiding in The Protector's garden fantasy or pretending to be in a piece of music? Gutless, spineless, nincompoops -- all of you! How many people do you think have nineteen voices in their head? No one! You are so messed up.

And you love your "Momma." What did she ever do for you? Don't think she didn't know what was going on? Why do you think she asked you if HE did anything to you? Wake up, girl. She was just as gutless as you.

Unlike the rest of you, I know who everybody is in our screwed-up mind and I make sure they all hear me loud and clear, whether they want to or not. I know, I know, all of you except the stupid little wimp, The One Who Never Got Hurt. I'll never understand why you don't let me get to her. I would tell her a thing or two and then some more.

You're right, I'm angry. I have a thousand reasons to be angry. What HE did to me for years was way beyond sick and HE said HE only "bothered" me. What a bunch of crap and nobody did a damned thing about it. Let's see? My aunt was "bothered" by HIM and she told on HIM when I was quite young. Was anything done about HIM then? No! HE raped HIS own sister and my so-called mother, and the rest of the family knew about it. Was anything done about HIM then? No! What was the matter with all those people?

And the pervert, HIMSELF. Did you ever think HE would say HE was wrong? NO! All HE ever said was, "Well, I know I was a bad father, but don't you be a bad daughter now." What kind of rubbish is that? HE wasn't a "bad" father, HE was not even a father at all -- just an extremely twisted PERVERT that managed to get away with it.

If you think you know anything about me now, you are wrong. Nobody knows anything about me and I don't care. I hate the world, I hate life, I hate HIM. Just go away and leave me alone.

164

12 The Liar

Lessons in lying
I was taught by the MASTER of lies.

I hated HIM
I hated HIS lies
I hated lying
but according to HIM,
I had to tell HIS lies.

HE taught me,
"Say this
don't say that
your story is going to be . . . or else!
I'm only teaching you things you'll need to know
when you grow up.
You don't know anything about love
and for certain
you know absolutely nothing about
sex.
You know you're my special girl
I love you
You'll see how much this will help you."

All lies
HIS lies
I hated HIS lies.

To be sure
I told HIS lies
HE put fear, lots of fear
way down deep inside my soul
where it scared me the most.
So deep and so thick was
the fear
that it could not be forgotten.

When HE thought I needed to tell one of HIS lies,
HE knew exactly how to extract the fear
from the pit of my soul with little more than
a certain raise of HIS eyebrow.

All lies
HIS lies
I hated HIM
I hated HIS lies
I hated lying,
but I told them anyway.

Stone-Cold Manipulation -- Stone-Faced Lies

While I have absolutely no recollection of how she got there, unfortunately, I will never forget taking my friend, Gwen, home. It was very cold that night and it had started to snow heavily around seven o'clock in the evening. At about eight, the phone rang and HE answered it. It was Gwen's folks calling to say she needed to come home; HE offered to take her. Smart enough to know better, I promised myself that I would never let HIM take any of my friends alone in the car. HE would probably try to "bother" them and I would end up forever and completely humiliated and embarrassed.

This night was no different; I insisted that I had to go along. Gwen and I sat in the back seat innocent and unconcerned about the weather or the short mile-and-half ride to her home. We chatted like girls will, going on about this and that and nothing in particular. In just a few short minutes we were there. We both said, "Goodnight. See you at school tomorrow." When she got out of the car, I got out too and moved to the front seat of the car for the quick ride home.

Instead of stopping at our house, HE kept on going and made a right-hand turn at the next corner. Instant panic attack -- up this road a few blocks and around another corner was an undeveloped wooded area, no houses, and several dead-end roads. I blurted out quickly, "Dad, why didn't you stop at the house? Where are you going? What are you doing?"

There's no place to hide, no place to hide. I'll have to get out of the car and run when HE stops. I am afraid I won't be able to run very fast in the deep snow. I don't have boots on, and where am I going to run to in this terrible winter weather?

Why are you so completely stupid to go along for this ride. You should have known better than to take a chance of being alone with HIM. You are an idiot!

167

What am I going to do? What am I going to do? How can I escape this? I'll run away.

As soon as HE stopped at the end of the dead-end road, *The Runner* was ready to go. I pulled on the handle I had been anxiously holding onto and jumped out of the car. I slipped a little in the snow and even before I was at the back end of the vehicle, HE was there grabbing at me. I fought really hard; I kicked, punched, scratched, and struggled until HE overpowered me and dragged me back into the car. HE yelled at me and told me to settle down or HE'd have to use his belt. While holding onto me with one hand, HE began pulling off HIS leather belt with the other. I was still kicking and screaming the entire time.

"No, Daddy. No, Daddy. Please don't do this. Why can't you be a normal father. I hate you. I hate you so much. Please don't do this. Please, Daddy, please!" I pounded on HIS chest and pulled at HIS hair. Finally, HE folded HIS belt in half and raised it over my head as if to strike me.

HE yelled again, "Are you going to settle down now or am I going to have to beat you with this?"

"Please, Daddy, please don't. Just take me home. Please take me home!"

I continued to beat on HIS chest and then HE turned me over and started beating on my back and buttocks, all the while saying, "As soon as you shut up and be still, I will stop beating on you. Shut up! Shut up!" After I had had enough beating, I quit struggling. HE immediately turned me around, unbuttoned my shirt, pulled up my bra, unzipped my pants, pulled them down, pulled my panties down and undid HIS pants . . . .

Even though the car was running, I remember being so cold. Shivering, I turned my gaze away so I did not see HIS transformed eyes, so I did not see what HE was doing.

An Inner Fantasy

I saw the lights of the dash board and The Protector came and took me to the safe place. I was in a fanciful dream. The Protector, an angel-like lady, had led us to a beautiful flower garden where the flowers and bushes were bigger than we were, an excellent, safe hiding place. When we got there, I would watch from my hiding spot in the bushes on the outside of the safe place, looking in at The One Who Never Got Hurt. She walked around busily tending to her flower garden, which was filled with white, pink and fuchsia peonies, translucent lemon and deep red, waxy begonias, and huge pansies that each held a purple angel, whose billowing wings and skirts lived within the brilliant yellow petals. While there were many other varieties of flowers in the flower garden, her favorite was the lavender-colored, giant garden phlox. There were hundreds of tiny lavender petals that made giant, beautiful flower heads which were so tall she didn't even have to bend over to smell them. Each petal felt as soft as a kitten's ear to the touch and smelled so wonderful that she could have lived in there forever.

The One Who Never Got Hurt was always safe and protected in my dreamy hiding place. Over in the distance she sees an original hand-hewn log cabin that hosts a large front porch with white pine furniture, whose cushions are covered in a fabric that captures the beauty of all of the flowers she loves so much. When she sits on that porch in the evening, she looks out upon a meadow stretching far across the horizon until the meadow meets the lofty mountain range that rises up at its edge. The sun kisses the mountains goodnight at the end of each day as it begins its nightly journey beyond the tall peaks to capture all of the brilliance it will need to illuminate tomorrow. Although the sinking sun only lightly brushes the mountain tops, they reveal to the orb the overwhelming awe of the earth's mystery that had been seen throughout the tranquil day. The sun's warm and colossal heart bursts open into a kaleidoscopic sunset that falls sparkling like diamond star-dust snow on top of the highest peaks. The magnificent mountains are instantly renewed and begin flashing and twinkling brightly as if flirting with the zillion tiny stars in the sky, beckoning them to come a little closer as night fills the sky with marvelous mysteries.

Each day the sun returns with a new sense of vigor, painting the firmament in a hue of blue more beautiful than the day before as it nobly rises higher and higher above the meadow. There may be a few clouds that float by in a myriad of shapes, forms, and subtle tints of colors, but they give The One Who Never Got Hurt something to do as she lies in the softest of green grasses looking up toward the heavens, contemplating the meaning of her existence. Once in awhile when she's curious, she'll take a walk out in the meadow which surrounds her home. If she wanders far enough, she will eventually come to a peaceful, meandering stream that is lined with thousands of colorful, smooth pebbles that sparkle from the star dust that had been washed down with the melting sun-kissed snow. The source of the pure-water stream seems to be a waterfall bursting high out of the side of one of the mountains. As she wanders up the side of the stream to get a closer look at the foamy waterfall, she usually watches a busy squirrel or little bunny doing cute squirrel or bunny things. Being tired from her long walk, The One Who Never Got Hurt lies down at the edge of the mountain's forest feet, which have made a super-soft, pine-needle bed for her to take a little nap upon before she returns home. While she sleeps, The Protector watches over her with unwavering allegiance, ever keeping her safe from harm, safe from memories, safe from HIM.

The One Who
Never Got
Hurt

4.3.98

171

Shivering and so cold, I heard HIM saying, "Jackie! Jackie! Button up now, get your pants on, and straighten yourself up!" As HE was getting HIS own clothes back on, HE said to me, "You are Daddy's most special and oldest girl. There are certain things that young girls need to know that only their daddies can teach them. When you are married, your husband is going to expect things from you, and that is why Daddy must do these things to you. So you can learn and be prepared for your wedding night. Boys are of the opposite sex and are very different from girls. They have needs and drives that are very powerful and girls have to really watch out for them because they'll want to do things with them before they get married. Now, that would be all wrong. You must watch out for these dangerous boys and not let them touch you or let them ask you to touch them until you are married. I'm just trying to teach you what you need to know. Right now you don't know anything at all about life and love, lust and sex, but just remember what I am teaching you and stay away from those dangerous boys. They are very different from girls and they are of the opposite sex. Do you understand this, Jackie? Now, mothers don't really like it that daddies have to teach this sort of thing to their daughters. So, it is best that you don't tell her about it. She will get mad at you for being a girl instead of a boy, and, as I said before, she will hate you. She will hate you so much that you won't have a family anymore. No one will love you if you ever tell -- not your mother, not your brother, not your sister, not your cousins, not your grammas, not your grandpas, not your aunts or uncles. No one will love you if you tell. Even your friends will hate you. Even though you desperately need to learn the things I'm teaching you, nobody else wants to know that I am teaching them to you. I know it's kind of weird, but that's just how it goes. So, you won't tell anyone about my lessons now, will you? Besides, it's just a little something you will need to know anyway when you get married, and even though it's a bother, there is no need for you to get all worried about it.

Don't tell anyone, okay?"

"No Daddy, I won't ever tell. I promise!"

"I don't know why on earth you have to cry so much and make your eyes all red and swollen like that." HE was exasperated with me. "You know I'm only trying to teach you things you'll need to know when you get married, and there is absolutely no reason to cry over it. Get your clothes on now, and I'll think of something for you to tell your mother when we get home. Oh, come on, Honey. Come here, let me hug you. You know I love you. You are Daddy's special little girl. You are so pretty, but not with those big red eyes and those huge crocodile tears. Here is a handkerchief. Blow your nose and pull yourself together now. Everything will be okay. Just stop crying, Sweetheart."

He continued, "Okay, this is our plan. As soon as we get home, you'll head straight for the bathroom, lock the door, and wash your face off with very cold water. In fact, hold the cold washcloth over your eyes for a little while. Then go right to your room and go to bed. But if your mother happens to see you and asks you about your red-swollen eyes, this is the story you will tell her. You'll say that you and Gwen were sitting in the back seat of the car as we drove her home, and the two of you were goofing around. Right before she got out of the car, she just poked her fingers as hard as she could right into your eyes. It hurt so badly that it made your eyes tear up immediately, and then you started crying because you didn't know why your best friend would do something so mean to you. Okay, Jackie, have you got the story now? Repeat it to me for practice. Okay, I think we're ready to go home."

When we walked into the kitchen from the garage, Momma was sitting right there waiting for us. I think we had been gone a long time considering the short trip it was to take Gwen home. She said something to HIM as I tried to make my way to the bathroom, which was on the other side of her. She reached out to me and didn't let me pass. She had noticed my red and swollen eyes immediately. She then did something that seemed strange to me. She took both of my arms in her hands and faced me eye-to-eye. She grabbed me hard and almost seemed to be shaking me. She then asked, "Did your dad do something to you tonight?"

I said, "No, Momma, HE didn't. Gwen was very mean and poked me in the eyes with both her fingers, and it really, really hurts and burns."

Jackie, are you telling the truth?" Momma said, continuing to question me.

"Really, Momma, that's what happened. Why would I lie about a thing like that? Gwen poked me in the eyes, and it really, really hurts." I started to cry again. "Why would she be so mean to me? I'm her best friend!"

HE stood straight and tall, right behind Momma with HIS arms crossed, HIS eyes glaring down at me, warning me, pulling up the fear from the depths of my soul so that I would tell HIS lie. I could not let her know what had really happened while we were gone. If she knew the real truth, she would hate me. I loved Momma and she must never hate me and never leave me. I knew I had to be believable, so HIS lie became my truth.

As I stood there watching her face and eyes as she questioned me, I wondered: *Why is she asking me these questions? Does she suspect something? Oh, please, Momma, know something and see the real truth in my eyes, even though I can't make it come out of my lips! Please see the truth, Momma, and make HIM stop doing this to me. Don't hate me and leave me either. I love you and need you so much.*

Finally, she accepted HIS lie that I told as the truth and let me go. I washed my face, went to bed, thinking about all of HIS lies until I fell asleep. I hated HIM, I hated HIS lies, I hated lying but I told them anyway.

The Happy One

People frequently would say:
"Smile, Jackie."
"How come you're so glum, Jackie?"
"Cheer up, Jackie, it can't be all that bad now."
"What's the sad face all about?"
"Cat got your tongue?"
"Do you ever smile?"

The Angry One always wanted to scream right back at them,
No, I'm not happy you stupid idiot!
I am living with a sexual maniac that I absolutely hate
because HE can't keep HIS sick hands to HIMSELF.
Of course, the rest of us wouldn't let her do that.

While the other ones became immediately energized
when they had a specific job to do,
like hide, run, lie, be smart, pretend, protect,
The Happy One was very illusive and seldom alert.
We all needed to be relaxed,
to be completely certain and satisfied
that HE was not a threat to us
before we could let down
 our guard
to make room for her to be.

From time to time,
always when HE was gone away,
we let go of our constant vigilance.

Then, The Happy One would come out to play
and for awhile she could
just be
a young kid, roaming free.

She took the brief moments whenever they came.
But when our guard was back up,
in her place was shame.
Happiness was a feeling that other people experienced.
For us, there were too many things to watch,
too many tears to cry, too much shame to bear.

A Summer Friend

Even though she had been in some of my eighth grade classes, and I thought she was a nice girl; I didn't know Samantha very well. In my mind she was a very smart, popular girl that was with the "in-crowd," always busy planning dances or running for student government. But there she was at the swimming pool all by herself on a cold and cloudy Wisconsin day in early June. In fact, she and I were just about the only ones there, and since we knew each other, we began talking a little as we took turns bouncing off the diving board. It was a good thing there was no line because it was very cold standing all wet and dripping in the brisk air. We practiced jack knives, backward dives, and swan dives, attempting to leave only a ripple in the water surface like the diving divas we were striving to emulate. However, we laughed at each other when we tried to do flips because we would make huge, embarrassing splashes. When we slammed into the water with the most ungraceful forms, we would be bit by a million stinging needles of water on our backs or stomachs. It started to rain, but the lifeguards let us stay anyway after we begged and pleaded with them for awhile.

They said, "Okay, as long as it doesn't start lightning."

Before long we were laughing and swimming and having a grand time in the big pool all by ourselves, ducking under water every now and then to escape the rain that continued to come down while we played. It was also warmer in the water than in the cold air. Samantha was a cheerleader so she suggested we make up a cheer for the rain. We worked out our little routine in the water, practiced a little, and told the lifeguards to watch us do our cheer. As we did our movements in the water, we yelled:

"Some say rain, rain, go away.
Why not say, rain, rain, please, please stay.
Come on down, come on down, we don't care, we're all wet.
Everywhere, everywhere!"

The lifeguards whooped and hollered with us, "Yeah, Yeah, Yeah!" Then, they told us they believed we had drunk too much pool water and it was making our brains silly. We laughed some more and went back to our play.

For the rest of the summer, we went swimming almost everyday, rain or shine. If we weren't swimming, we were sitting on the living room floor with our cards spread out all over the place, playing a huge double-deck rummy game that Samantha had taught me. Throughout that summer I was sleeping over at her house or she was at mine. She also played the piano, so every once in awhile we'd find a duet piece and play music together. In her upstairs room, we'd sit on her bed to look through magazines and pick out our favorite coolest and cutest singers or talk about high school coming up. We went shopping together and did all those things young teenage girls do. I was enjoying my new friend and the carefree summer just like any other ordinary, happy kid.

When Samantha and I returned to school at the end of that summer, our former circles of friends were there to greet us. We talked with each other a couple of times the first day or two and then an uncomfortableness started to form between us. While the words remained unspoken, we both knew our close friendship had come to an end. We lived in different worlds in the halls of school. Even though we were respectful and kind to each other, offering a smile or quick greeting, we never hung out together again. I don't know if she was sad, but I was very sad. She had given me the happiest summer up to that point in my life. Often I wondered if she knew how much I wanted to remain her friend. *The Shy One* always watched her closely over the next four years and longed to be like her, to join her in all of her activities, but *we* couldn't do it. It simply was not possible.

I don't know where HE was, I don't remember HIM being around very much, and HE did not "bother" me once that entire summer.

14 The Shy One

So afraid to speak
so afraid to look at a boy
so afraid to participate in anything
that might involve the "cool people"
so afraid a teacher would call on me to answer a question.
So afraid, so afraid, so afraid.

I silently watched while the world was
doing.
I felt like a non-participant, a non-person,
as if I lived in the wall
to more closely observe the movements and actions of others,
of HIM.
I was so afraid of HIS movements and actions.

If I was silent and still,
I could study people's faces,
I could study their words,
I could study even the finest minuscule details of their movements
to know better what they might do next,
what HE might do next.
I was so afraid of what
HE might do next.

I wanted to relax
I wanted to say what was on my mind,
the words simply would not
come out of my mouth.
I was so afraid to speak.

I wanted to be like the other people,
laughing and talking,
enjoying activities,
enjoying each other.
I was so afraid to let my guard down.
So afraid, so afraid, so afraid.

I wanted to just
be
without always
being so afraid.
I wanted to
feel
what it felt like
to be a normal person,
I was so afraid that would never happen.

Being so extremely shy was so
extremely painful.

Blocked Words -- An Inner Dialogue

Open your mouth and say the words . . . movement of the throat to speak . . . nothing comes out . . . blockage . . . words are stuck down in throat . . . can't make it past uvula . . . throat closes down on the words . . . sends them back . . .

Oh, why is this so hard? . . . just a simple question . . .

It's okay, think about what you want to say, try again . . .

I can't, the words won't come out . . .

You are such a stupid little ninny, too afraid to ask a simple little question . . .

I can't make the words come out . . . I open my mouth and the words won't come out . . . tense shoulders . . . tight neck . . . headache . . . confusion . . . stare at fingers . . . bite fingernails . . . crack knuckles . . . rock back and forth . . . stomach hurts . . . Oh, why can't I make the words come out . . . Pressure in my head . . . seeing double . . . press eyes wide open . . . eyes bulging out and hurting . . . pressure behind eyes . . . bite on fingers some more . . .

Try some deep breaths, breathe in, breathe out, take a deep breath . . . relax . . . What do you think will happen if you ask this one simple question? . . .

I don't know . . .

Nothing will happen, you will ask the question and it will be answered . . .

Maybe it would be better to wait until another day? . . . I really don't need to know the answer today . . . I think I know what the answer will be, so why should I ask? . . .

Oh, come on, you can do it, you can, I know you can . . . You are an intelligent and smart young lady, you certainly have the right to know the answer to your question today . . .

But I am so dumb I can't even make words come out of my mouth . . .

Yes you can, I know you can . . . open your mouth and say the words, it won't hurt . . . just do it . . .

Okay, form words in throat . . . up they come . . . there is a blockage . . . the words won't come out . . .

Oh my God, I don't believe her . . . she's not going to ask the question today. I don't know why you all keep trying to get her to do it . . . she's so afraid to talk, so afraid someone will tell her something she doesn't want to hear . . . so afraid something bad will happen . . . you are a scaredy cat . . . cat's got your stupid tongue again . . . too bad for you . . . too bad for you . . . yeah, that's right, chew on your fingernails some more until they bleed . . . at least you will know you have blood in your veins and you're not a dead zombie . . . zombies don't talk you know . . . just like you, they ain't got no tongue . . .

Listen, I am going to ask this question today if it's the last thing I do . . . somehow I will make the words come out of my mouth . . . I just have to . . . I have to prove her wrong . . . I am not a zombie . . . I do have a tongue . . . I am not a stupid idiot . . . I can do this . . . I am not a scaredy cat . . . nothing bad will happen . . . rocking back and forth faster . . . pain in my eyes . . . seeing double again . . . feeling sick to my stomach . . . feeling like I need to throw up . . . Why is it so hard to ask a simple question about something I'd really like to know?

Just relax, Sweetheart, and breathe deeply . . . don't worry so much about the question or the anger . . . just relax . . . it will all be okay . . . you don't have to ask the question . . . it doesn't really matter in the grand scheme of things . . . life will go on whether you ask this question or not . . . just relax . . .

"Momma . . ."

"Yes."

". . . Um . . . Um . . ."

"Yes, Jackie?"

"Oh, never mind" . . .

There you go, you got something to come out . . . that's a start . . .

But I didn't ask the stupid question . . . Why didn't I ask the question when I had her attention? . . . Now I have to get her attention all over again . . . this shouldn't be this hard . . .

No, it shouldn't, you nincompoop . . .

Don't start on me again . . . rocking back and forth . . . chewing on fingernails again . . . headache . . . bad headache . . . all around the top of my head, like there is vise-grip on it . . .

Close your eyes for a moment . . . relax . . . breathe . . . breathe . . . okay, try again . . .

"Momma . . . "

"Yes."

"Um . . . "

"Go ahead Jackie, what do you have to say?"

. . . "Um . . . When" . . .

"Yes"

. . . "When can I start dating?"

She smiled and said, "Oh, probably in a couple of years when you are fifteen or so."

"Okay."

Like you will actually ever go on a date . . . ha, ha, ha . . .

Well, at least she asked the question.

Why did it take you an entire hour to ask that stupid question anyway?.

I don't know . . .

Why does it take you an entire hour to ask any stupid question?

I don't know . . .

What's the matter with you?

Nothing's the matter with me . . . go away and leave me alone.

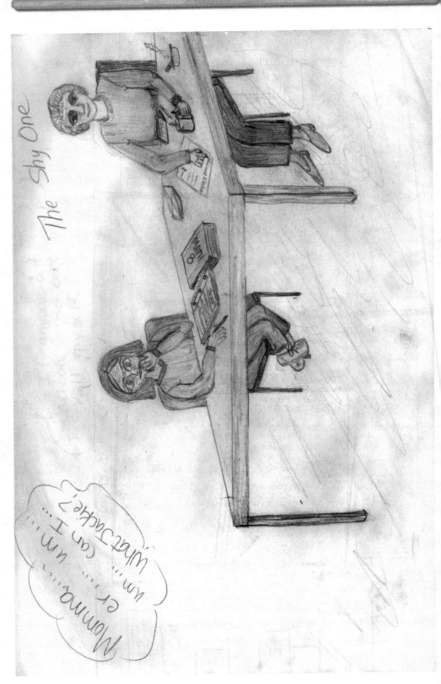

The Newcomer and Uncle Timothy

They hadn't been married very long. Lori was very tall, slender, and only nineteen; but she was a grown woman that had the most amazing eyes. I watched them closely as they twinkled merrily with a warm glow of inner peace, confidence, and happiness. There was no mistaking it, she was the most beautiful individual I had ever been lucky enough to see up close in all of my twelve years. Not only was she extraordinarily pretty, she was also extremely sophisticated and skilled -- she had an office job. She was a secretary, took shorthand dictation from her boss and typed letters, which seemed to be highly respectable work according to my relatives.

In spite of their admiration for her work talents, they made fun of the way she walked and talked. Taking turns, my mother and her sisters would imitate her, trying to determine who could do it best. They would take a lot of time to position a cigarette just so in the fingers of their left hands, their elbows bent up just like she did and slightly held out away from their bodies. Next, they would proceed to walk across the room, grossly over-exaggerating the swing of their hips, stop, turn, mimic her smile, and say something she would say, like, "Timothy, darling, would you please give me a light? Thank you, you are such a sweet man." Then, they would all burst out in laughter at her supposedly quirky habits. I didn't understand why they mocked her; I figured they were just jealous of this gorgeous, worldly, and cultured newcomer to the family. Personally, I thought she was one of the nicest persons in this sourpuss family; at least she smiled and talked kindly to me, instead of yelling at me.

It was a summertime weekend again and there were a lot of visitors at Grandpa Jameson's farm. Even though Timothy and Lori were among the ranks of the married folks, they were on the very bottom of the seniority list. Therefore, they were assigned sleeping quarters in the little house along with us kids.   Without any objection from us, they claimed the bed in the tiny bedroom at the back of the house and since we weren't used to them sleeping in bed "together," we privately giggled about it with each other. Several of us kids were also assigned sleeping quarters in the tiny bedroom, but we were put on the floor at the foot of the bed.

After everyone quieted down and we were presumed to be asleep, I heard Lori laughing quietly. She said to Timothy, "Get out of there! We can't do that, not with all these kids in here.

He said, "Come on, Honey, they are all asleep and won't hear a thing." Then I heard them kissing, covers moving, bed creaking sounds, and quiet moaning. They said, "I love you," kissed each other some more and when everything became quiet again, I went to sleep.

Why did the grownups decide I should go home with Timothy and Lori to spend a week with them? I don't know. Perhaps because I was not very good at saying no. (Oh, excuse me, *The Angry One* just reminded me, because I was incapable of saying no.) I went home with them Sunday evening.

The plan was that I would stay there with them all week and Uncle Timothy would drive me home the next Friday night after work. As we drove along on the way to their house, the unfamiliar countryside passed by quickly outside the back window of the car. I wondered what I was supposed to do all day when they were at work. I smiled a little to myself when I remembered what I had heard the night before, daydreamed about the time when I would have someone to kiss me, and thought about how I was rather embarrassed about what they might have been doing up in that bed.

When we arrived at their extremely clean home, Lori made supper for us. She very politely showed me where everything was in my bedroom, where the towels were in the bathroom, what to eat for lunch, how to work the TV, and suggested I read some of her collection of *Nancy Drew* books.

Because *The Angry One* was mad at us for not saying no, because *The Shy One* was so very shy, because *The Ugly One* felt extremely ugly in the presence of this model-like, lovely, grownup woman, and because *The Dumb One* felt stupid next to this smart, up-and-coming office secretary, we didn't have much to say. Mostly we felt uncomfortable while they were home and answered whatever questions they asked with a nod of the head or a very meek yes or no, never offering any conversation *ourselves*. With bewilderment, I would study their faces and their movements, carefully watching how they interacted with each other.

I had never been around a newlywed couple before and found it very interesting to see how they were always holding hands, offering each other kisses and hugs, how they managed to get so tangled up in each others' arms and bodies while they watched TV, and how they would gaze deeply into each other's eyes with a secret understanding that only they were privy to. Lori seemed to enjoy being close to Timothy and accepted all of his touching with a warm fondness.

Our routine was the same every day. Each morning about six o'clock, Lori would get up and make breakfast for the three of us, and lunch for Timothy and herself. While she was doing that, Timothy got dressed and ready for work. After breakfast, he was on his way out the door by about 6:45 a.m. They would stand together in a prolonged embrace, holding each other closely as he kissed her goodbye for what seemed like a very long time, and then he left for work. Next, Lori would get herself ready to go. Sometimes I would stand in the bathroom and watch her put her makeup on -- she seemed very good at it. One morning while I was doing this I mustered up enough courage to tell her jokingly that she was an artist at work. In the evening when they came home, I watched them hug and kiss each other so sweetly and discuss how their day's work had gone. Lori would fix supper in the evening, we would sit down together to eat, wash dishes, watch TV for the rest of the night, and go to bed around ten o'clock.

The week went by rather uneventfully and I was as bored as I imagined I would be, sitting there all day by myself. The only good thing about it was that I wasn't anywhere near HIM and didn't have to worry about whether or not HE would try to "bother" me. Regardless, I was glad when Friday came and I could go home.

When they arrived from work on Friday, I was packed and ready to go. Lori insisted, however, that we have supper before we left. Just as planned, Timothy would drive me home. We said goodbye to Lori right after supper and off we went. If I were uncomfortable with Timothy and Lori together, I was even more uncomfortable with just Uncle Timothy. I sat as far over as possible on my side of the car and didn't say anything for almost all of the two-hour drive home. Timothy would make attempts at conversation, but all I would say was a curt yes or no. When we were about forty-five minutes from my home town, Timothy reached his hand over to me and started rubbing my upper thigh.

He asked me, "Do you like the way that feels, Jackie?" He moved his hand a little farther up my thigh, and started to rub more in between my legs. "How do you like that? Is that better? Does that feel good? I bet you would like to learn all about sex, wouldn't you? I bet you are ready to start 'doing it,' aren't you?"

Speechless, I didn't know how to respond or what to do. *The Angry One wanted to fly off the handle and start beating on the guy. The Smart One said that might not be a good idea since he is driving the car and it could cause us to end up in an accident. The Shy One couldn't say anything, all of the words were stuck somewhere between her head and her tongue. There certainly was no place to hide or to run. So, we just sat there very stiffly, with some sort of dumb look on our face.* He kept this up for about two minutes. I don't know how long for sure, it might have been one minute or ten minutes, but it seemed like an eternity. All I knew is that I was scared, that I wanted him to stop, and I couldn't make any words come out of my mouth.

Some more time passed and he said to me quizzically, "Jackie, isn't that shortcut around here somewhere, you know the one that cuts over to Camp Phillips Road? Do you know where that is?"

I lied. "No, I don't know where that road is," as we drove right by it. *He must have thought I was crazy -- there was no way I was going to show him where that road was. It was a back road, a secluded area where there would be no traffic at all. I wasn't going to be that stupid with the way he was talking and had been touching me before.*

As we neared my house, he said to me, "Jackie, please don't tell anyone about me touching you, okay? They will probably blame you for letting that happen. You won't tell, will you? Will you?"

Being very embarrassed about it all, wondering how he could do this to me when he was just newly married, and feeling bad for Lori, who obviously loved him very much, I snapped back at him as we pulled in the drive, "Don't worry, Uncle Timothy, I won't tell anyone!" I was home now and that was all I cared about.

SECTION IV:

THE HIGH SCHOOL YEARS

    Instead of being the carefree, happy years of youth, high school was tortuous for me and became much more so by the time I was a senior. I had a very low self-esteem, I was extremely shy, and could not wait to be finished with school.

15 The Dumb One

Dummy, Dummy, Dummy.
Jacque is a Dummy.

You're damn right you're dumb
You are the queen of dumb
You are her highness of dumbdom.

You win the top prize for being dumb.
Only someone as dumb as you
would hang out for years with
someone who constantly told you
how dumb you are.

Dummy, Dummy, Dummy.
Jacque is a Dummy.

16 The Smart One

123, ABC, You can do it,
yes sir-ee.
I see Jane, I see Dick
reading, writing, 'rithmetic
all well done, grades will show,
take a bow, way to go.
Some may think I am me,
but we have hid, we are me.

The Hider hides, the Runner runs,
the Liar's lies have just begun.
Don't be fooled by Anger's bark,
and dear poor Shy One has no spark.
Some may think I am me,
but we have hid, we are me.

When Sad is sad, and Dumb is dumb,
The Truth comes out when we are done.
Protecting and Pretending was one way
we were Held Together day-by-day.
Some may think I am me,
but we have hid, we are me.

Pretty or Ugly, who really knew
The One Who Never Got Hurt, that's who.
Happy and Sex went hand-in-hand to our
 Musical-make-believe-you-are-whatever-you-want-to-be Land.
Some may think I am me,
but we have hid, we are me.

Jesus, Jesus, dear Lord, she prayed
The Religious One was never frayed.
The Smart One figured us out
just how, who cares, we won't pout.
Some may think I am me,
but we have hid, we are me.

Wrapped tight or not, you have seen
a young girl's scheme
to reach her dreams.
Nineteen in all, we are me
much better and stronger we can be.
Some may think I am me,
but we have hid, we are me.

The Queen of Dumbdom

Early in elementary school I learned that if I worked very hard my teachers would treat me better. Doing my best was not an option; it became a dire necessity to my psychological survival because I so desperately needed praise, admiration, recognition and approval from someone. My wonderful teachers were always willing to give these blessings to me freely, so schoolwork quickly became a safe haven for me. Schoolwork completed well was an emotional investment which would yield me a sense of pride, a sense of belonging, a sense of accomplishment, a feeling of being worthwhile, and a feeling that I was good at something. All I needed was one kind remark written on a paper, one encouraging word, one pat on the back, and I was beaming inside. Doing well in school had its rewards and I capitalized on them as much as I possibly could.

Not only did I get the accolades I needed, schoolwork also gave me a place to hide. If I kept busy in my school work, others were not asking me questions or involving me in sometimes painful conversations -- painful in the sense that it would require me to speak. And remembering how shy, ugly, and dumb I felt, speaking was painful, especially if the speaking involved a dangerous boy or one of the pretty, popular girls. By the time I was a senior in high school, I could not even bring myself to look over to the row of desks next to me if a boy was sitting there -- I truly was that afraid of boys. It was much easier to busy myself in schoolwork, mentally tune out the others in the room, and avoid unwanted contact.

Consequently, I did rather well in school, except, of course, on the social level. I put in the time, I did the work required of me, and kept my silence as much as possible.

To survive the best I could, I invested all of my efforts into building a good friendship with one girl that lived a few houses down the block from my friend Gwen. I started to get to know Sara in eighth grade when we were in the same science class, and I'd see her when I went to visit Gwen in the evenings. Sara went with her family to their lake-side cottage for the summer, but once we entered ninth grade, we started to do everything together and became inseparable.

It was surprising how so many of the freshman boys had grown taller over the summer. I had been taller than most boys all of my life and here I was looking up at them. It scared me. It scared me a lot. Why? Because now they were almost all grown up, they were not little kids any more. They had hair on their faces, and some of them were obviously shaving; they had muscles, lots of muscles in their arms. And when we went to gym class and the boys were out on track field in their gym shorts, well, . . . they had hair all the way up their legs. Once in a while some of them would take off their shirts after running, and they had hair on their chests, too! That could only mean one thing, they must have hair "down there." These taller boys were, all of a sudden, different creatures. They were creatures of the opposite sex and God only knows what they might be thinking. HE told me they were "dangerous," these "boys of the opposite sex." HE said I should be very leery around them and watch out for their tricks because they might try to get me to have sex with them.

While the boys had changed over the summer, so had many of the girls. They were wearing eye makeup, some had dyed their hair blonde, and others had fixed their hair in a more fashionable style. Their nails were a little longer and polished with the latest colors. Some of them were wearing the newest styles in clothing. I didn't know how they could do it, but they were actually talking to the "dangerous boys of the opposite sex" and enjoying it! At lunch the girls would sit next to the boys, looking so relaxed and casually chatter nonsense with them as they ate -- they would laugh coyly and smile when the boys told jokes.

As the year progressed, I developed a little crush on one of those "dangerous boys," and I made the mistake of telling Sara about it. Late after school one night when no one was around, we sneaked into school, went by his locker, and I touched it. "Sara," I said, "this is Brian's locker!" As I touched the handle of the locker I told her, "Just think, he probably touches this handle fifty times a day, so that means his molecules are on my fingers right now."

She came over to me and said, "Let's open it up and see what he has in there."

Much to my mortification, hanging on one of the hooks inside the locker was a strange white, belt-like contraption of a thing that had an underwear band on it, but not much in the line of anything else that resembled boy's underwear. Unfortunately, I just knew somehow it had to go on "down there."

"What is this?" I said to Sara.

She grabbed it out of the locker, looked at for awhile as she moved the straps around in her hands and said, "It's a jock strap, you dummy. The guys wear it to keep their, . . . ah, . . . you know, . . . ah, . . . their thing from bouncing around when they play sports."

"Oh, I see," I said. "Well, put it back in his locker. You don't really want to be touching it, considering where it has probably been and all."

Instead of putting it back, Sara started running down the hallway with it.

I screamed, "Sara, bring it back here right now!" I caught up to her just as she was going to go down the stairs, and I grabbed one end of the strap, but she didn't let go. We stood there pulling it back and forth; the elastic would stretch her way and then my way as we were tugging and struggling over the awful thing.

"Sara, let go, we've got to put it back in his locker. Come on, Sara, let go!"

Well, she didn't let go, and, without warning, my end suddenly broke and went snapping back to her. When the realization of what had just happened sunk in, we both started laughing so hard that Sara peed her pants right there.

"Oh Sara," I said laughingly, "what are we going to do now? We broke his stupid jock strap!" And we laughed some more until we both had tears running down our faces. "I really think we should put it back. Give it to me and I'll go put it back in his locker."

Instead of giving it to me, she turned and ran down the stairs and flew outside. I followed her again and watched in horror as she threw it into an open art room window. There it was, the weird, white-strap-of-a-thing that went "down there" on a boy's body, laying right smack dab in the middle of an art room table. Brian A. was written on the waistband and was staring back at us with no way to retrieve it.

"Sara, why did you do that?"

She said to me, "Oh, don't be so dumb, Jacque. Whoever finds it in the morning isn't going to have a clue how it got there, and Brian will never know who took it out of his locker. No one will know it was us."

Right then and there I pledged I would never, ever have another crush on a "dangerous boy of the opposite sex" until I was far away from Sara; and if I did, I certainly wouldn't tell her about it. And for Brian (or any other boy for that matter), well, I never looked Brian's way again. I was just too embarrassed knowing what we had done.

Wherever Sara went, I went. Whenever I wanted to go someplace, we usually didn't go. It was okay with me as long as we didn't have to talk to boys. As our high school years went on, however, Sara became the more dominant one in our relationship. She was in charge, but we were best friends anyway. For some reason, she was constantly putting me down with a continuous litany of belittling rhetoric.

"Jacque, you are so dumb; you don't even know how to comb your hair, iron your clothes, shave your legs, fix your nails, have fun, or dress right; you have such a weird religion; you are so gross -- don't leave your orthodontic rubber bands on our table; you couldn't find another friend if you tried; there isn't a boy anywhere that will ever like you; why do you want to go to a stupid football game? Sometimes I wonder why I even hang out with you."

With Sara's unrelenting insistence and constant reminding that I was so extremely dumb, I grew to believe and accept what she said as the truth and began telling myself I was dumb. These feelings of dumbness and inadequacy grew worse and worse. By the time I was a senior, it was at its height. I believed I was totally dumb, totally stupid, totally unlikable and there was no way that a boy was ever going to like me enough to want to be with me. As for Sara, well, I couldn't wait for graduation day because after that I wouldn't have to be around her everyday and she wouldn't have to put up with me -- *Her Royal Highness, Jacque, The Queen of Dumbdom.*

17 The Sad One

Sad is such a small word for the
h u g e
ache in my mind that reaches every single molecule
of my being.

Melancholy.
Dark, oppressed, mournful, afflicted, miserable, troubled,
sorrowful, melancholy. **Sad**.

None of these words describe the
Sadness that permeates my entire being.

Dejected.
Depressed, despicable, despondent, dispirited, distressed,
discouraged, doleful, down, downcast, downhearted, dejected.
Sad.

Sad to the very d
                e
                   e
                      p
                        e
                          s
                            t
                              depths of my soul.
Forlorn.
Deserted, abandoned, pitiful, hopeless, desperate, gloomy, out of
place, cheerless, gutless, spineless, mirthless, voiceless, forlorn.
Sad.

Sadness oozes out of my tears,
Sadness oozes of my pores,
Sadness oozes out of my nose,
Sadness oozes out of my throat,
but no words come out.
There are no words to describe the
Sadness I feel.

Incurable.
Inadequate, inarticulate, incapable, incoherent, incomplete,
inconsolable, inconceivable, incurable. **Sad.**

Sadness that never goes away.

Unrelenting,
Unending, unmanageable, uncontrollable, unfit, uneasy,
uncomfortable, unconnected, unhappy, unbalanced, unknown,
unrelenting. **Sad.**

Sadness is always in my mind,
Sadness is always in my soul,
Sadness is always in my body,
Sadness always, always, always so **Sad.**

Panic Attack

There were occasions when I would come home from school to find an empty house, go to my room to change out of my school clothes, and HE, being completely naked, would burst out of my closet when I opened it. Of course, I would jump back and scream from being startled and from the fear of knowing what HIS intended purpose was. Because HE had managed to scare me so masterfully and catch me completely unaware, HE laughed wickedly with a sheepish grin of delight. HE seemed to enjoy scaring me this way, always staring piercingly at me with HIS evil-driven eyes. Where do you go when all of a sudden HE is right there in your room inches away from you, ready to grab what HE wanted. At times like these, when there was no warning of what HE was up to, I would frequently run to the bathroom and lock the door if I were able to get away. I remember fearfully standing on the wall opposite the bathroom door, or standing in the shower behind the shower curtain while HE was fidgeting with the lock, trying to open it.

Screaming loudly, I would say to HIM, "Go away, please go away, Daddy. Please don't come in here. Leave me alone. Just leave me alone." Other times I would hold my hand on the button of the locked door, attempting to re-lock it every time HE got it open. I was prepared to fight as soon as HE got in the room.

The Angry One, of course, would be yelling and screaming in my head. *Why did you come in here? That was so stupid -- you know HE always gets the lock opened, you know HE always gets in. Why do you continue to be such an idiot? You can't find a decent hiding place and you can't run away fast enough to save yourself. You are pathetic, absolutely pathetic. Look at your ugly self in the mirror. What a sorry excuse for a human being -- so stupid with your eyes all puffy and red, so scared -- just a scaredy cat. Dumb, dumb, dumb, that's what you are. No wonder HE's always after you -- he knows how dumb you are!*

Once he got the door opened, I would expend all of my strength beating on him, kicking, biting, scratching, trying anything and doing everything I could think of to free myself from his truculent clutches, until, finally, I didn't have any spirit left and HE'd overpower me. "If you don't settle down right now, I'll have to get the snakes again and teach you another lesson. Shut up and settle down." Or, "I can take my belt off and beat on you until you settle down. Now shut up!"

"Why do you do this to me, Daddy? How can you call yourself a Christian? You are the devil. How can you pray at church? How can you teach Sunday School? How can you serve on the church board? You are nothing, but a hypocrite -- the biggest hypocrite of all times! I hate you, I hate you so much. Please just leave me alone. Why can't you be a normal father? Why can't you love me the way a father is supposed to love HIS daughter? Why can't you just stop doing this? You are not a father at all, you are a monster. Please, Daddy! Just leave me alone!"

One day, during a scenario just like this one, HE stopped -- was fifteen years old. I have absolutely no idea what made HIM do that, but HE just stopped. HE promised me HE'd never do it again and HE didn't. HE hugged me and told me HE was sorry. HE said a prayer and never assaulted me again. Often I wonder why HE quit on that day. Was I too big for HIM to handle? Was I no longer little and not satisfying to HIS pedophilic desires? Was HE truly sorry?

Don't be fooled, I wasn't. HE didn't give up HIS evil ways. HE started assaulting my younger sister more frequently. I would hear HIM in the other room "bothering" Maria and now I had a new guilt to deal with. Because I was responsible for making HIM quit "bothering" me, I felt it was my fault that HE was "bothering" her more. Shame, guilt, hurt for Maria, and a secret, but painful comfort in knowing HE wasn't doing it to me.

I hate you, I hate you! Please, please don't do this to me. Just let me go, please let me go Daddy. Why do you do this to me? How can you say you love me and still do this? How can you say you love God? You lie to me and everyone else. Please Stop! Stop Daddy. Stop!
You kick, you bite, you scratch me, Now Knock it off and be still or I will have to get the snakes again to teach you a lesson. Be Quiet! Be still!
Not Strong Enough
Jacqueline

When I was entering my sophomore year of high school, Pastor John approached me about an idea he had. Somewhere along his way, he had met a few deaf people and felt a need to reach out to them. He proposed that he and I learn sign language together at the local technical college. After we became proficient signers, I could interpret his sermons by signing for deaf persons and he would minister to them. Of course, I said yes. Every Tuesday night for two school years he would faithfully pick me up at my house at six o'clock in the evening and off we would go together to learn sign language. Frequently, we would practice together before or after church or in the evening after school.

Spending time with Pastor John was so much fun, and as busy as he kept me, I spent a lot of time with him. He was a rather young, jovial Texan minister in his early thirties, who had moved to Wisconsin with his wife, Faith, to start a "mission" church. We loved to tease him about his Southern drawl which never wore off during his stay in "Yankee territory" as he referred to central Wisconsin. He was a small-framed man, maybe about five feet, nine inches tall with blond hair that was already beginning to show the first signs of balding; but I found him quite dashing. Bright blue, teasing eyes seemed to curiously peer deep into my eyes, as if to be searching for my soul. Once he found what he was looking for or knew he had my full attention, he would somehow touch me through his eyes and I could feel his unique brand of charisma vibrating through my mind. He quickly became the one and only man in the entire world that I trusted to always be upbeat and full of joy, predictable in temperament, and never had to worry that he may approach me in a sexual way; I was safe with Pastor John.

Over the years, I grew to love him deeply in many different ways. He was the role model for the male friend I would one day like to marry; he was the father I wished for and knew I would never have. He was always there to offer me encouragement and belief when doubt crept in about God's calling of me to be a missionary. In his actions, he taught me compassion, goodness, and fullness of faith as he shared with those around him. And he loved me in an appropriate way that a Pastor should love a young woman in his congregation. I held him in the highest regard and expected the highest standards from him. Looking back on my feelings for Pastor John, perhaps I expected too much of "the man."

I first noticed it when he had cried despairingly at every service at summer camp, the summer after my junior year in high school. I knew something was up, but I had no idea what caused him to be so sorrowful. Over the next several months, he continued to act strangely out of character, he fidgeted more, cried frequently during his sermons, and the teasing look in his bright blue eyes was seldom there. Then one Sunday in April of my senior year in high school, the pastor made a teary-eyed announcement to the congregation that he had accepted a call to serve as a minister at a church in Colorado. He would be leaving in early June shortly after school let out. This came as a disastrous and devastating blow to me.

No, this can't be true. He can't be serious that he is leaving here. What am I going to do without him? Why does he have to go? Doesn't he know how much he means to me and everyone else in this church? Doesn't he know he will leave a vast void in our hearts and minds when he goes away? I prayed to God for weeks, asking Him to change Pastor John's mind, but God didn't answer this prayer.

On a Saturday afternoon a few weeks after his announcement, Maria came running into our house screaming that HE was fondling her. In a dumbfounded and dazed, despondent shock, I went flying to my room and locked the door immediately.

No! No! Maria, how could you do this? Don't you know what torment and wretchedness is going to happen to us now? We are going to be abandoned, left to fend for ourselves in our own terror, agony and misery. This is a catastrophe, the biggest catastrophe of my entire life! How could you do this, Maria? Oh, my God! What if she tells someone else? They'll find out about it. Oh, my God! Appalling humiliation. I can't believe she told Momma. No! No!

Catatonic panic attack, outraged, anguished, terrified, petrified, traumatized, and horrified -- how could she do this to us? What am I going to do? I have to hide, I have to run, I have to lie. We will lie if they ask us anything. No, HE never touched us. No, never. Really, HE never did anything to us! I don't know what she is talking about. No. Never! Never! Never! Oh, my God! Heaven help me. Heaven help me. This is the worst day of my life, worst day of my life. What am I going to do? Eventually, I cried myself to sleep.

The next few minutes (or was it days) were nothing more than a tormenting blur. Momma was knocking on my door.

"Jacque, I want to talk to you. Jacque, are you in there? Jacque, open the door. Let me in, Honey. Pastor John is here and he wants to talk to you and Maria."

Oh, my God! She told the minister. How embarrassing, how humiliating, how degrading. Why did she have to tell him of all people? Why? Who else will she tell? Oh, my God! What if she tells all the relatives and they all know? I'll never be able to look at anyone again.

Out in the living room there sat Pastor John, Maria, and my mother.

"Jacque, did your dad ever do anything to you?"

Silence, complete silence . . . havoc racing through my mind . . . *mustn't tell . . . mustn't tell anything* . . . they said other things to me, what the words were I have no idea. *The Shy One* couldn't talk, no words would come out. *How long have I been here?* I tasted salty tears on my tongue and wiped the snot away

216

from under my nose as I frantically rocked back and forth. Their lips were moving and they were looking at me, but I didn't hear what they said.

Finally, and after what seemed like an eternity had passed, HIS lie came out of my throat.

"No! HE never did anything to me. I don't know what you are talking about!"

"Well, Maria said HE was fondling her body and bothering her. Did HE do anything like that to you?"

"No! Never. I don't know anything about what HE did to Maria, but HE never did anything like that to me. Never. Can I go back to my room now? I want to go to my room."

Pastor John said, "Let's pray together first."

He prayed something, I have no idea what he said. Then I ran back to my room, locked the door, flung myself onto my bed, weeping in despair over the burdensome events that had just happened, and cried myself to sleep once again.

Sad couldn't even begin to describe what I was feeling that next Monday morning when Sara and I hurried into school because we were almost late again. We didn't speak.

As if it weren't already bad enough that my mother and HE were getting a divorce, now my minister and everyone else in the entire family knew about what HE had done to Maria and me. What if anyone at school finds out -- I would kill myself. They must all know already that my parents are getting a divorce. No one else's parents are getting a divorce, it is so disgraceful. Just a few more weeks to graduation and I won't have to come here to this agonizing place ever again. I won't have to pick up Sara every morning for school or see her at all if I can help it. Sometimes I just wish I was dead.

Why couldn't HE have been a normal father? Why couldn't HE have loved me like a father is supposed to love HIS daughter? What is the matter with HIM? What is the matter with me? I am so ugly, I am so dumb, I am so shy. I can't do anything right. Why was I even born? God must hate me to let all this happen to me. When I was little, I must have done something really bad and God has punished me all these years for that one sin. I wish I had a different father, a different life.

People look at me weird, they must think I am really pathetic. I am so afraid they will see what HE did on my face. I must always look down to make sure they don't look at me too much and see IT. No fun to be with, always so sad, nothing to say. Pathetic, pathetic, what a pathetic excuse for a human being I am. Taking up space, taking up air, no good for anything, that's me.

Talk to no one, look at no one. Do what has to be done and leave. That is what I am going to do today. No one wants to talk to me anyway. I am just a boring, sad person with nothing to say. Even if I did have something to say, it wouldn't come out of my throat anyway. I don't blame them for not wanting to be my friend. I am just a boring, sad person with nothing to say.

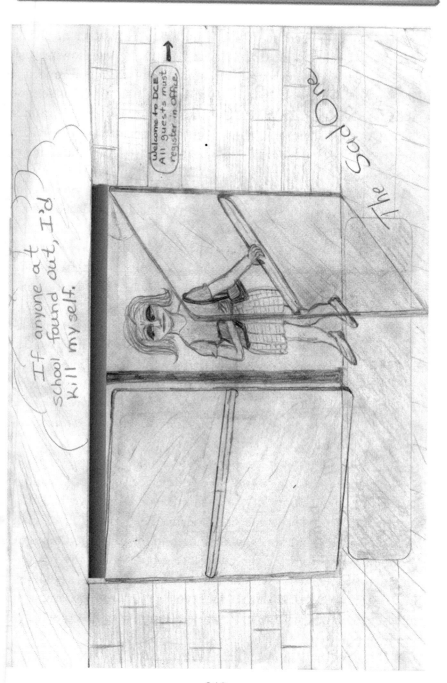

I have no idea how long I remained in a state of shock. Most of that entire time frame is just blank; and following that afternoon meeting with Maria, Momma, Pastor John and myself, I had been unable to look at or speak to Pastor John. I was much too embarrassed about what he might think of me, and I had no idea what anyone else had told him. I guess HE had talked to Pastor John too, crying and begging forgiveness in prayer, but I never believed any of it for one second. Without a doubt, I knew that whatever the MASTER OF LIES said to Pastor John, ninety-nine percent of it was not true. Certainly I hadn't told the Pastor anything about HIM.

One evening just before he was going to be moving away, Pastor John called me to ask if I would go out for an ice cream with him to say our good-byes. I felt I needed to go to say a special goodbye to one of the most important persons in my life and I accepted his invitation. At the very first moment I stepped into his car, I started to cry and never quit the entire evening. There were so many things I wanted to say to him, but nothing would come out . . . *Lump in throat, blockage . . . why can't I say what I want to say? Here my pastor is leaving and I can't even tell him what he has meant to me all these years . . . so much to say and nothing will come out of my throat . . .* so, just tears.

Pastor John never ran out of words to say, but that night he rode in silence for a long while. We got our ice cream cones and he chatted idly about some of the memories of things we had done together and I tried to smile and nod my head, still full of tears. When we finished our cones, we returned to his car to go home. As he turned away from the direction that would go to my house, I thought privately to myself that he knew I wanted to say things. Since I appeared to be unable to say what was on my mind, he probably figured if he drove me around long enough it might give me enough time to get the words out.

Then, Pastor John started talking about HIM. He asked

about HIM, and I could not talk about that, so I just cried more. As he continued talking about HIM, I stopped listening. I didn't want to talk about HIM, not with Pastor John, not with anyone. All of sudden I hadn't any idea where we were. I didn't recognize anything and it seemed like we were driving on a rather remote road. I suddenly wondered where we were going and I got scared. A few words he was saying began to reach me.

He said, "Why . . . just think . . . your father . . . teach . . .?"

Anger welled up in me and to my surprise, a strong, "What?" came out of my lips.

He repeated, "Why don't you just think about what your father was trying to teach you? Forget about anything that was bad and just concentrate on the good things that came out of HIS lessons."

Oh no, I thought to myself. He thinks HE actually taught me something! HE didn't teach me anything, nothing at all. He doesn't have any idea what I went through. What did HE tell him anyway -- lies about how HE taught me things I'd need to know when I got married?

Then, Pastor John reached over and touched my body somewhere. I don't even know where, but the touch was unmistakably, a sexual touch. Fright and surprise raced through my mind and my body. At the same time, Pastor had a different look in his eyes, and he said softly, "Jacque, what did HE teach you? Can you use that knowledge with other people?"

Oh my God! He thinks I learned how to have sex and now he wants to have sex with me! Oh my God! How can I get out of here. No where to hide. No where to run. No, this can't be happening, not Pastor John. No.

Pulling away and looking down ashamedly at my feet, all I could do was cry some more. I had trusted Pastor John and now HE ruined that trust. It's HIS fault. I hated HIM for corrupting my

Pastor and destroying the only decent relationship I had ever had with a man.

Sensing my reaction to his touch, Pastor John moved his hand away. He said nothing, but seemed to be starting the car in another direction.

When we pulled into our drive, I was still crying. All the words I wanted to say swarmed like stinging bees through my mind, never making it anywhere near the blockage in my throat, never even pretending to form on my lips, remaining unspoken forever. If I hadn't been betrayed, I might have been able to say, "I'll miss you. Thank you for everything you ever did for me." Or, "Please don't go, I love you, my friend, and you mean too much to me." The only words that came out were, "Goodbye, Pastor John," as I quickly jumped out of the car when it stopped, ran into the house, and locked myself in my bedroom.

After he and his family moved away, there it was. The tremendous emptiness in my heart that I had feared, uninvited as it was, had arrived anyway. Disappointment, loss of a friend, death of an innocent belief in man and religion, discouragement, grief, and pain remained with me. Not only had I lost my minister and dear friend, but all of the memories of our time together were now appallingly obscured by a dark stain of betrayal and thoughts of sin. Carelessly planted in my pastor's mind by HIM and HIS lies, he let the idea of sin grow out of control and reached out to me to carry out the act that had been nourished by EVIL itself.

In that one brief lustful touch, my faith was shattered into a zillion laser-sharp pieces that ripped through the very foundation of my beliefs. When the plunder and pillage of my soul was complete, the remains of my Christian conviction were torn to shreds. I was extremely disoriented, and *Anger* was in a very rebellious mood.

18 The Sexual One

HE said to me,
You know absolutely nothing about sex
You are so young, so innocent, and have so much to learn
Life, love, marriage, sex, babies.
Do you understand? Do you understand?

Be careful around "dangerous boys"
They have needs and desires you won't like.
When you have sex with a man, you are married to him.
He will want you to do things to him you may not like.
Do you understand? Do you understand?

When your husband wants you to do things to him
You must do whatever it is that he wants.
You know absolutely nothing about sex.
Do you understand? Do you understand?

I wish I had said to HIM,
Stop! Stop!
I don't want to know what YOU have to tell me.
It isn't true, I know it isn't true.
Do YOU understand? Do YOU understand?

YOU know absolutely nothing about sex.
Just what do YOU think YOU are teaching me?
That a father can use HIS daughter
as if she were an object?
Do YOU understand? Do YOU understand?

Dangerous Boys? I'm too afraid to look at a boy
let alone allow him to touch me or me touch him.
Do YOU understand? Do YOU understand?

How can YOU tell me about love and marriage?
If this is how a man loves HIS wife and family,
I don't want to know.
Do YOU understand? Do YOU understand?

YOU know absolutely nothing about being a father.
YOU know absolutely nothing about me.

When my family is all away, I try on Momma's nightgown,
her high-heels, a little lipstick, rouge, and perfume too.
Strut around room, swinging hips back and forth, look in mirror,
I know more than what HE thinks I know about sex.

Boobs are growing, see them bulge
a little when I bend over, and what
a butt -- nice, firm and round.
I know more than what HE thinks I know about sex.

Tingles down there, just a little bit
of hair growing there,
touch myself, wet, rub myself and it tickles,
differently.

I know more than what HE thinks I know about sex.
Someday, someone will come along
that I will want to kiss, hug, squeeze, and have good sex with,
kiss mirror for practice, mmm, am I a good kisser?
I know more than what HE thinks I know about sex.

He will be different from HIM.
He will be slow, gentle, and patient with me.
He will love me and make me happy.
I know more than what HE thinks I know about sex.

There will be no suffering in this perfect love.
No pain, no hiding,
no running, no lies,
no anger, no pretending.

I'll be able to forget about HIM
I'll be able to forget about HIS lies.
I'll be able to forget about HIS threats.
I know more than what HE thinks I know about sex.

You Are So Beautiful

Parked on a lonely back road somewhere on a moonless summer night, we were in the back seat of his car. He was young, strong, and handsome; and his kisses were so wonderful and so sweet, even a little wet. Looking into his dark eyes, so close to mine, I saw his love for me. I was enjoying being kissed and being held so close. Finally, I had someone of my own to hold me with his strong arms in a tight and close embrace. This handsome young man kissed me and made me feel like I was someone really special. I needed that after Pastor John left my life.

Then he does something that catches me by total surprise. He reaches for his pants, unzips, and takes IT out. The snake like thing with one eye. He wants me to touch it, but I am afraid of it.

I quickly draw back, and the handsome young man says with a chuckle, "It's okay, it's not as if it's going to bite you. Just touch it, touch it just once. Go ahead, touch it. Here, give me your hand and I'll help you."

Actually, I wanted to vomit my guts out right about then, but I let him take my hand and he put it on the awful thing. But I quickly pulled my hand away like a cat that is withdrawing its paw as it toys with something it just found on the floor. He put his hand back on mine and told me to try again. I touched it a little longer, stroking it with one finger, getting to know it a little bit. He asked me to put my fingers all the way around it and then to move it up and down a little; he showed me how. Then he moaned a little and I thought, oh boy, this is it, this is enough, and I quickly removed my hand. I told him I wasn't ready yet.

He said, "Oh, come on, Honey. I want you. You are so beautiful and my thing is all big and hard. I want you, I want to feel your body close to mine."

I said more firmly, "No, I am saving myself for the one I am going to marry. I want to go now. Take me home!"

Reluctantly, he put IT back in his pants. We crawled back into the front seat, and silently drove home. Then he kissed me good night and left. *The Angry One chided, you shouldn't expect anything from any man except that he wants sexual things from you.*

I had just been introduced to the first man in my life that actually took "no" for an answer about a sexual matter -- talk about a major surprise. Also, I had just been introduced to consensual sex as an adult, not that I knew anything about consent and sex in the same sentence at that time. I just knew what HE taught me; and HE taught me that, if I ever did have sex with a man, that man will be married to me. Sex and marriage were synonymous with each other. It's not that it was that much different from anyone else's fatherly advice, it was just the way the message was delivered. Just like the messenger, the message was extremely perverted and all mixed up in my mind. Sex was not the beautiful precious activity shared between two committed people. Instead, sex was a hideous act, which was accompanied by pain, fear, terror, and an entire host of other awful emotions.

In my eighteen-year-old eyes, the beautiful young man was perfect in every way. I had met him years ago when our families went to square dancing lessons on Sunday afternoons. Because there weren't any other young people in the group besides both of our sisters and his little brother, we ended up as dancing partners quite frequently. One good thing, I believed, about the situation was that he was from a different school. We went to Saturday afternoon matinees when we were in sixth grade and we went to another movie once when we were both fifteen. Over the years we saw each other at square dances too. It was always exciting when he would ask me to dance with him. Right after our senior graduation, he called and asked me if I wanted to go to a movie with him, and I decided to go. Talking with him was not too much of a problem. Even though I was shy, he managed to keep the conversation going because we did have some history, we knew each other's families, and we had some things in common to talk about.

After the movie date he asked me out again, and then again. Before long, we were seeing each other almost every night and I was falling in love for the first time. He kept the pressure on about having sex and by the end of August, he had managed to convince me to do it. The first time we did, I told him several times during the act, "Do you know what this means? We are married now! We're married! I am your wife." I don't know for sure if he just accepted that fact, or if he just went along with the flow because he was happy getting what he was getting. Regardless, about one year later he gave me a ring and we started planning our wedding.

There was one problem though, the young man was Catholic and I was a Baptist, albeit a disillusioned Baptist. Since he came from a family of devout Catholics, his mother said the only way we could be married was for me to become a Catholic. Of course, I decided to do it, and Momma had a fit. She begged me and pleaded with me not to change my religion and not to marry him. She had my former Sunday School teacher come and talk to me. And then she had my Southern Baptist minister come all the way back from Colorado to try to convince me I was making a mistake. Little did they know that in my mind I was already married to the handsome, young Catholic man. It didn't matter what they said, the deed was already done and there was no way to undo what God had already joined together.

At that time in Wisconsin, eighteen-year-olds could purchase beer, but not other alcoholic beverages. He had some good friends that we would get together with to play cards, socialize, and drink beer. So I joined the crowd. I quickly learned that alcohol was a soothing remedy for whatever ailed me -- shyness, dumbness, ugliness, or feelings of anger -- I liked the way it felt.

While I was not completely wild, I had done a fairly good

job of turning away from most of my former beliefs. I was converting to Catholicism, I drank beer, I was fornicating with a handsome young man that would be my legal husband before too long, and I wouldn't have to me anywhere near HIM. Life was going to be okay.

I thought to myself, *I am going to be happily married and we will have a wonderful life, I know it, I just know it.*

19 The One Who Holds Us All Together

The rest of my stories are locked inside,
the key was thrown away.
just be.

You mustn't come here, you mustn't insist
and you can be sure that I will resist.
The warning alarm I always keep
sounds off loudly when I am afraid
you'll dig too deep.
just be.

I have done my job, I have done it complete
the answers you seek, I will not repeat.
The answers you seek are not mundane,
the answers you seek will drive you insane.
So go away my child, let the questions be
for the answers you seek are not for you to see.
just be.

Too busy to talk, too burdened to tell,
too dark to know, too evil to remember,
don't bother me, I have a job to do.
just be.

Beyond the Darkness in Our Mind -- An Inner Dialogue

Once in awhile many of the other children will come to me. They want to go beyond the darkness in my mind. It isn't all of them, just a few of the more curious ones that say to me, we have no fear, we can handle anything. Maybe if we face what you know, we can become more healed, more whole.

Yeah, if we get it out in the open, we can all deal with it!

I tell them, you don't want to go beyond the darkness in our mind. Just believe me and go away. I promise you, beyond the darkness in our mind is certain insanity for all of us.

The most frightened ones usually stand in front of me and tell the others to go back to their own places. I scare them. They do not want to know what I know, what darkness lies within.

When you are ready, you will know more, but only little bits and pieces at a time. We cannot survive all that is beyond the darkness in our mind -- it is locked up in there on purpose. It is there to maintain our equilibrium, it is there to protect us. It is there to keep the deepest, most evil, most horrific experiences out of our conscious mind forever. There lie the most unspeakable horrors, the deepest, darkest, and most frightening things that we have ever experienced. Some things that we must not remember, not now, not ever.

Remember what happens when we dig too deep. We all get scared, we all get confused, we all get frantic. And then, I can't keep us balanced. You all start yelling and screaming at me, you all want answers, you all want peace to be restored. You must not push me. It is not good for me to get overwhelmed. I do not talk much, I don't need to. I just need to be left alone to do my job. I have no more stories to tell you for this book.

You out there, whichever one of you is writing this story, just quit now. Please, just go away and leave me alone to do my job. I must watch and not let my guard down by your wanting to write this silly book. Go away. What I do is dangerous and it is not good to get me thinking too much. Go away, go back to living, not remembering. Trust me, you do not need to remember what I know. You do not want to know what lies beyond the darkness in our mind.

Epilogue

Laboring through a slow and painful recovery process, I was able to unravel and recognize the resiliency, innovation and intelligence of my vulnerable, terrified, and young mind to mentally survive in a frightening, unfathomable reality. When I started to exhume my past in therapy sessions, the *voices* became panicky, agitated, and frenzied. Trying to figure *them* out seemed to give some of *them* a much larger *voice* than *they* usually had. The adhesive, yet precarious equilibrium was disrupted and all of *them* started screaming at me. The ensuing mental chaos seemed like I had an entire uproarious Greek theatrical chorus in my head, ringing out complaints and emotions, demanding and questioning why I was resurrecting those ghastly memories that tormented *them* so. I was not used to this and it was quite unnerving. Eventually, I learned that an important part of *our* delicate balance is not to dwell on all *our* different *voices* too much, but at the same time listen to *their* wisdom and what *they* are telling me about how to take care of my emotional needs. With the aid of several excellent psychologists and wonderful treatment programs, I was able to calm my *voices* and balance was restored.

While it took me twenty-plus years after leaving my childhood home, I finally was able to put the pieces of my troubled past together. I found a lasting peace within my mind, and yes, the *voices* are still with me. I teach at a high school, I have two wonderful sons in college, a great step-son and daughter-in-law, and I am married to a very good man. I enjoy working in my flower gardens, playing the piano, and lead a very ordinary, quiet life.

Like many others, I had come to believe that God had forsaken me long ago. As I matured, however, I realized that God does not interfere in the actions or choices that a person makes. Just as we have a free will to choose goodness, we also have a free will to choose wickedness. Unfortunately, HE chose wickedness.

I believe I have let go of the hatred I once felt, but I have chosen not to be in a relationship with HIM. If I could, I would have HIM put in jail, but that is no longer possible due to the statute of limitation laws in Wisconsin. Many people have told me, "Jacqueline, you must forgive HIM. After all, HE is your dad."

Finally, someone came along and said that it is okay not to forgive HIM, and this person was a minister. What a relief! If you could put yourself in a similar position, would you be able to forgive someone that repeatedly sexually assaulted your little girl, not once, but a hundred times? Probably not, not even if it had happened only one time. Being given the permission to not forgive HIM was a huge burden lifted from my spirit. The minister said, "Who are we to forgive someone of sin? That is God's job, not ours."

When my sister-in-law heard my story, she gave me a Bible verse that has meant a lot to me:

"Do not fret because of evil men, or be envious of those that do wrong; for like the grass they will soon wither . . . give yourself to the Lord, trust in Him and He'll help you. He will make your righteousness shine like the noonday sun!" Psalms 37

In our "civilized" society, commonly found statistics show that one in three girls and one in five boys fall victim to sexual assault, in some way, before they reach their eighteenth birthday by a perpetrator she/he already knows. Tragically, only a very small fraction of these assaults are ever reported to the police. Obviously, this is one area we are not effectively addressing as parents, teachers, or churches. Even though the subject matter is extremely sensitive, I strongly urge you to discuss these atrocities with young people and adults in your care. Tell them about the long-term damaging affects a sexual assault has on its victims. It doesn't just last a few minutes, the affects can last a lifetime. With the ever-increasing display of violence, promiscuity, nudity, and sexuality permeating our lives on television, in our music, and other media, the need is greater now than ever before.

My message for those of you reading this book that are currently or were victims of evil deeds or unfortunate circumstances is to remember that you are not alone. The shame is not yours to bear and you **_must_** tell someone that will listen and then seek help to heal your wounds. Just as Sarah said to me, "I want you to go forward with your life and I believe you will only be able to go forward by first going back. What you really need to comprehend is that what happened to you, while it is all over and done with, is so much more than just a few memories -- you suffered severe emotional trauma. Even though the wounds can't be seen they are there, buried deep in your mind. These wounds are festering in your spirit and are affecting you today. You won't get better by just ignoring your past because it's too agonizing to reminisce." You do not have to go at it alone, and it is not a sign of weakness to ask for help -- it takes a courageous person to admit help is needed. There are many trained, professional mental health therapists that are ready to assist you. Find someone that you are comfortable with that has a lot of experience in dealing with your specific issues.

For those of you who are in a position to counsel such victims, but are not trained in dealing with a specific type of trauma, do them a favor and refer them to someone who is trained. Poorly trained counselors, while having good intentions, did not help me. In fact, several persons disappointed me so greatly that I left counseling for years, delaying any possibility of healing. A true professional, be it a high school guidance counselor or nurse, a minister, a therapist, will know the limit of his / her expertise and will not hesitate to do what is best for the individual.

If you are a perpetrator, a pedophile, reading this book be aware that you may keep your victims silent when they are little, but you won't have control over them forever. They do grow up; they will go away from you; and eventually, they will tell. Some of them will tell when they are little; you will be found out and jailed, as you should be. Hopefully, legislators will realize the inability of young people to name their attackers and will lift the statute of limitations so that criminal charges can be brought against you many years after the crime has been committed. There are programs available to help you with your sickness. Seek help before ruining a child's life.

Finally, a plea to members of the clergy. Never, never, approach one of your parishioners on a sexual level, be it a child or an adult. All it took to completely destroy my faith for years was one sexual touch -- just one touch, nothing more. He did not follow through with any other actions or suggestions, he never brought up the subject again. But one brief sexual touch on my body caused vast havoc in my soul. I can only imagine what a full-fledged assault would do to someone. It can destroy an individual. Once discovered, it can cause an entire church to lose faith. And it could completely destroy the chance of ever reaching those that have left their church because they were already discontented.

If I can leave the reader with an encouraging word, it would be this. As much as we would like to believe we have complete control over our destinies, we don't. However, no matter what anyone did to us in the past, no matter what happens to us in the future, we, alone, choose how to react to whatever comes our way. We can choose to use life circumstances to make excuses for our own poor behaviors, or we can choose to be our best in spite of them. We can choose goodness.

You can choose goodness, you can, I know you can!

Resources

National Women's Health Information Center
1-800-994-9662; 1-888-220-5446 (TDD)
http://www.4woman.gov/violence/index.htm

Division of Violence Prevention
Centers for Disease Control and Prevention
http://www.cdc.gov/ncipc/dvp/dvp.htm

The National Sexual Violence Resource Center
1-877-739-3895

Rape, Abuse, and Incest National Network
1-800-656-HOPE

National Center for Victims of Crime
http://www.ncvc.org/

National Domestic Violence Hotline
1-800-799-SAFE or 1-800-787-3224 (TDD)
http://www.ndvh.org/

Pennsylvania Coalition Against Rape
125 N. Enola Drive
Enola, PA 17025
1-888-772-PCAR
717-728-9740
717-728-9781 (Fax)
http://www.pcar.org

Stop It NOW! (child sexual abuse)
413-268-3096
413-268-3098
http://www.stopitnow.com

http://www.mftsource.com   Click on Crisis

Books on Healing

Affirmations for the Inner Child by Rochelle Lerner

Alcoholic's Anonymous by Alcoholic's Anonymous World
Services, Inc.

Beyond CoDependent No More by Melody Beattie

Bradshaw on the Family by John Bradshaw

CoDependent No More by Melody Beattie

The Courage to be Yourself by Sue Patton Theole

The Courage to Heal by Ellen Bass and Laura Davis

The Courage to Heal Workbook by Ellen Bass and Laura Davis

Feathers on the Wind by Edward Hays

The Giving Tree by Shel Silverstein

Healing the Child Within by Charles Whitfield

Healing The Shame That Binds You by John Bradshaw

It's Never Too Late to Have a Happy Childhood by Claudia Black

The Language of Letting Go by Melody Beattie

Oh! The Places You'll Go by Dr. Seuss

Parenting With Love and Logic by Foster Cline, M.D. and Jim Fay

Soul Survivors by J. Patrick Gannon

tuesdays with Morrie by Mitch Albom

The Twelve Steps by Alcoholic's Anonymous World Services, Inc.

Twenty Four Hours a Day published by Hazelden

When Bad Things Happen To Good People by Harold S. Kushner

The Woman's Book of Courage by Sue Patton Theole

References

p. 154   Excerpt taken from *The Holy Bible*, The Lord's Prayer and John 3:16

p. 154   Excerpt taken from song, *There's Just Something About That Name*, by William J. Gathier and Gloria Gathier.

p. 155   Excerpt taken from familiar hymn, *This Is My Father's World* by Maltbie D. Babcock, 1858 - 1901 and Franklin L. Sheppard, 1852 - 1930.

p. 155   Excerpt taken from familiar hymn, *In My Heart There Rings a Melody*

p. 155   Excerpt taken from familiar hymn, *Just As I Am*, by Charlotte Elliott, 1789 - 1871 and William B. Bradbury, 1816 - 1868.

p. 155   Excerpt taken from familiar hymn, *Amazing Grace*, by John Newton, 1725 - 1807.

p. 155   Excerpt taken from familiar hymn, *Sweet Hour of Prayer*, by William W. Walford and William B. Bradbury, 1816 - 1868.

p. 155   Excerpt taken from familiar hymn, *Holy Spirit Be My Guide, by* Mildred Cope, 1924.

p. 155   Excerpt taken from familiar hymn, *It Is Well With My Soul*, by Horatio G. Spafford, 1828 - 1888 and Phillip P. Bliss, 1836 - 1876.

p. 240   Excerpt take from *The Holy Bible*, Psalm 37.

Sexual Assault Statistical Web Sites

U.S. Department of Justice, Bureau of Justice Statistics
http://www.ojp.usdoj.gov/bjs/abstract/saycrle.htm

Sexual Assault Statistics
http://www.familiesincrisis.net/sexual_assault_statistics.html

Department of Student Life, Texas A&M University
http://studentlife.tamu.edu/gies/SexViolence/rapestat.htm

National Center for PTSD (Post Traumatic Stress Disorder)
http://www.ncptsd.org/facts/specific/fs_female_sex_assault.html

National Organization for Women
http://www.now.org/issues/violence/stats.html

United Against Sexual Assault of Sonoma County
http://www.uasasonoma.org/html/nationalstats.htm

Healing Music

During some of the most difficult and painful moments throughout my recovery process, the music of these two artists quieted, soothed, and calmed my troubled spirit. I highly recommend these CDs for their healing potential and therapeutic qualities.

Each CD is only $15.00

Dan Hansen—Piano   Jeff Pockat - Ancient Wire Strung Harp

Add $2.95 shipping and handling for each CD.
Wisconsin Residents add 5.5% Sales Tax.

Call Toll Free (888) 493-3719
FAX No. (877) 876-3807

To mail your order make a list of the CDs you want. Enclose your list with a check or money order made payable to I Have A Voice Enterprises. Or, you may charge your order to your credit card by sending us the information shown below.

Payment Method:

_____ Check/Money Order Payable to I Have A Voice Enterprises

_____ Mastercard   _____ Visa   _____ DiscoverCard

Signature _____

Card No. _ _ _ _ - _ _ _ _ - _ _ _ _ - _ _ _ _   Expires _ _ / _ _

I Have A Voice Enterprises
P.O. Box 83
Peshtigo, WI 54157

How To Order Additional Copies of this Book

You may order additional copies of *The Hider's Story* ($12.95) and the *Companion Journal for The Hider's Story* ($9.95) by calling or completing the order form shown below. FAX or mail it with your check / credit information to:

I Have A Voice Enterprises
P.O. Box 83
Peshtigo, WI 54157
FAX No. (877) 876-3807
Phone Message No. (715) 789-2793
Call Toll Free (888) 493-3719

For large quantity discounts and/or wholesale information, please call or FAX the number of books you desire, along with your contact information to the respective number shown above and a representative will call you to discuss your order.   Thank you.

$2.95 shipping and handling for each book.
Wisconsin Residents please add 5.5% Sales Tax

_____   Check or Money Order Enclosed
_____   Mastercard _____ Visa _____ DiscoverCard
Signature _____

Card No. _ _ _ _ - _ _ _ _ - _ _ _ _ - _ _ _ _   Expires _ _ / _ _

Visit our Web Site for copies of drawings from *The Hider's Story*, and other related products: www.thehidersstory.com
Watch for the next book of Jacqueline's trilogy:
Finding The Rainbow House
The story of the handsome young man in her life.